The Small Business Digital Marketing Playbook

How to Attract and Retain the Next Generation Customer

By

Walter Lis

The information presented herein represents the views of the author as of the date of publication. This book is presented for informational purposes only. Due to the rate at which conditions change, the author reserves the right to alter and update his opinions at any time. While every attempt has been made to verify the information in this book, the author does not assume any responsibility for errors, inaccuracies, or omissions.

Contents

Preface

Digital marketing is a fast-growing industry; with nearly ninety percent of all purchase decisions beginning online, connecting with consumers in the digital world has become the principal strategy to efficiently scale business growth. I wrote *The Small Business Digital Marketing Playbook* to fill the tremendous need for a practical, no-nonsense guide for small and medium-sized businesses to the growing digital marketing industry.

For the past twenty years, I've been involved with building websites, growing audiences, and attracting customers online for businesses ranging from multi-billion-dollar companies to sole proprietorships. The companies I assist represent a wide variety of industries including media, publishing, telecommunications, manufacturing, local government, information technology, construction, and finance.

My passion for creating and executing successful online marketing strategies leverages my technical skills within SEO, paid advertising, email marketing, social media marketing, and web analytics. My core technical skills include web programming, graphic design, writing and editing.

With a background in statistics and big data, I take a data-driven, pragmatic approach to digital marketing that provides scalable growth through an emphasis on optimization and testing. As digital marketing continues to evolve at a frenetic pace, I believe that testing, discipline, and continuous education are the linchpins of success for all online marketers.

I've been able to use my varied organizational experience to help target and identify strengths and weaknesses within digital marketing programs. The net effect of this approach is cutting-edge opportunities and solutions that may originate in one industry and work even better in another.

This book has been written to help you to understand how all the components of digital marketing work together, and how the devilish details within each component need to be aligned to become a finely tuned machine for lead generation, lead nurturing, and business development. The book gathers my diverse technical skills, creative abilities, experience, and state-of-the-art industry knowledge to help you assess online opportunities before building and calibrating your digital marketing strategies and components into a highly profitable revenue source for your business.

**FOR THIS BONUS
ONLINE CONTENT VISIT**
walterlis.com/resources

To help you put these strategies into action, I've included the above button throughout the book to identify when related online content is available. On my website (walterlis.com/resources), there are 20+ lists containing links to the latest digital marketing tools, software, platforms and service providers.

Instead of including these lists in the book, I chose to post them online so they can be updated on a consistent basis. As I discuss in the book, the digital marketing world changes quickly, so having this content online will help us keep these resource lists relevant.

Chapter 1

The Rise of Digital Marketing

Like never before, the information economy has brought power to the customer. If a consumer is looking for information, they can turn to their smartphone, computer, or a countless number of digitally connected resources to instantly get information on what they're trying to buy, fix, or accomplish.

This digital revolution is no more evident and impactful than for small and medium-sized businesses (SMBs), which are generally defined as those businesses having fewer than five hundred employees. Over the past twenty years in the United States, the percentage of SMBs has dramatically increased. According to the Small Business Administration, SMBs make up 99.7 percent of employers in the United States. Small and medium-sized businesses make up 64 percent of net new private sector jobs. SMBs number 27.9 million, as compared to 18,500 companies with 500 employees or more. That's a huge number, and these enterprises have a major impact on the global economy.

So what does that mean for SMBs when they need to compete with larger businesses in the new information economy? It means major opportunities!

The power of the information economy is translated across all demographics into nearly all segments of the marketplace, where we are seeing a rapidly growing digital audience. Even for those who didn't grow up with this type of technology, the information revolution is becoming a major part of their lives.

According to the United States Census Bureau, 78.9 percent of all US households owned a computer in 2012, and 94.8 percent of households with a computer use it to connect to the Internet. This includes devices such as laptops, touchscreen tablets, smartphones and gaming consoles.

Pew Research has reported that as of April 2012, 53 percent of American adults ages 65 and older use the Internet or email. This is a dramatic surge from August of 2008, when just 38 percent of adults ages 65 and older were online.

In addition to increasing adoption rates across all age groups, the popularity of smart phones has continued to grow exponentially, providing an entirely new audience for small and medium-sized businesses. According to the 2014 Pew Research Center Internet Project Survey, fifty-eight percent of all adults have a smartphone. Among age groups, eighty-three percent of ages 18-29, seventy-four percent of ages 30-49, forty-nine percent of ages 50-64, and nineteen percent of those 65+ use a smart phone.

Even more telling is the changing focus of all US Internet usage from the desktop to mobile. According to a study by comScore, in January of 2014 Americans spent 46.6 percent of their total Internet time with mobile apps, versus 45.1 percent who accessed the Internet via a desktop computer.

With this increasing mobile acceptance and growing audience comes great opportunity. Nowhere is this more evident than for small and medium-sized businesses as their customers become more digitally enabled and digitally focused.

At the same time, response rates across all marketing channels have been shrinking. That means not only billboards, display ads, and other types of traditional media have seen decreasing responses, but most digital forms of marketing and their responses have as well.

Small and medium-sized businesses need to have a plan to reach this digitally connected audience, and they need to provide themselves with all the necessary tools and information to cut through the clutter and sell their products and services. While this is a great challenge for SMBs, it's one that has to be met head-on.

What does this mean for the marketer? It means that while we are in an increasingly competitive environment, it's one that can be successfully managed if you have a plan and systems in place to help take your business to the top.

There are many reasons why the challenge of marketing has become more difficult, including a host of new channels as well as many more options and opportunities for distraction. But it doesn't mean that any of these opportunities should automatically be avoided. Consumers have more information and nearly all their answers at their fingertips—and it's your job to find those fingertips.

In addition to finding the consumer in this congested marketplace, and reaching them with the proper message, there are numerous new opportunities that all of this evolving technology has provided. The audience and communities created by social media channels allow marketers the chance to reach their potential customers in their own neighborhoods. Marketers today can now search for and find leads in a variety of new ways that were not available a few years ago. This changing of the guard, and the opportunities that come with it, is happening at a rapid pace. Therefore it's up to the marketer to keep track of all that is going on.

One of the primary benefits of digital marketing is its ability to construct a cost-effective approach to building an audience and attracting leads. However, without the proper system and processes in place, the exact opposite can occur. An organization can waste a great deal of time, money, and opportunity cost trying to put together a scattered or fragmented digital marketing plan, with limited or diminishing returns.

However, when executed properly, digital marketing can allow for the scale and growth that is necessary for small and medium-sized businesses to transform their organizations. The importance of a properly developed program within the digital realm is that it can allow a small and medium-sized business to compete with an organization of any size.

The reality is that while small and medium-sized businesses must continue to compete with larger organizations, the playing field has been leveled. Many of the tools and advantages that a large organization typically could enjoy because of greater resources are muted in the digital realm. This technological and resource equality presents many opportunities for small and medium-sized businesses to grow like never before.

A question that I often receive when meeting with businesses is what is a realistic timeframe for an organization to see results with digital marketing programs. As you might expect, the answer to that question can be tricky, because it depends upon multiple variables and lots of different internal and external factors.

However, a balance can be achieved between the efforts put forth within a digital marketing campaign and the fruits of this labor that directly reflect how well the program is put together. This means that a better organized, more thought-out, more defined program is likely to bring about much more widespread, impactful and faster results.

So how does digital marketing fit within your business? The reality is digital marketing is now just marketing. Your email marketing, your social media marketing, your paid digital advertising, and your search engine optimization are now all components of your traditional marketing program and should be managed as such. A new and constantly changing skill set is required to be able to manage these components; however they must interact with the rest of your marketing program. Having a digital marketing campaign on its own island will negate many of the benefits that a solid digital/offline combination program can produce.

Mindset

One of the aspects of digital marketing that has always appealed to me is the idea that the tools, elements, and factors within digital marketing allow for constant improvement. Inherent within your digital marketing toolset will be feedback on nearly every data point, both internal and external.

The magic with this is that we can learn from what we've done, and from what our audience, leads, and customers have shown us.

Marketing is a continuous process, not a destination; and "set it and forget it" is an idea that is well past its time. Every campaign and every program that you put forth across all channels within digital marketing has to be constantly improved. This also means that those of us working within digital marketing, whether you are a full-time marketing professional or you're an owner of your own business, must be able to change and adapt with this fluid environment.

Virtually nothing stays the same within digital marketing, from Google's search algorithm, to social media network changes, to the way email hosting companies assess deliverability. For example, according to digital marketing tools provider Moz.com, Google changes its search algorithms as many as five hundred times per year. With all of these changing variables, it's essential that a digital marketer be willing and able to adapt and constantly improve.

In addition, each channel has its own set of constantly evolving rules and boundaries that have to be followed. For example, within search engine optimization there are a number of rules, or best practices, such as the use of link title tags and original content. If you break these rules or proceed against what the search engines are looking for, you'll get unsatisfactory results and you'll have less traffic to your website.

Within social media, each channel has its own rules and best practices. Whether you are on Facebook, LinkedIn, Twitter or any other social media channel, there are a number of terms and conditions that each of these channels has established. Their goal for these rules is to protect their customers and their businesses, and it's your job to follow their program.

To keep up with the need for ongoing improvement in response to constant changes within digital marketing comes the need for continuous education. We have to continue building our skills and expertise to stay competitive. However, it's very difficult to be an expert in more than one area of digital marketing. And with an extremely wide breadth and depth of skills and expertise that are necessary for success, it's clear that you need a system in order to accomplish your marketing and business development goals.

Who Should Manage Your Digital Marketing?

To cope with the wide array of knowledge necessary for the role, we often use the term "T-shaped marketing skills." This basically refers to having modest knowledge in a broad array of skills, and deep knowledge or ability in a smaller set. For example, if you have extensive expertise in email marketing and copywriting, then that would be your middle "core" skill, and you'll look to maintain a secondary amount of knowledge and information about the other topics.

However, since your core "T" strength is email marketing, you'll probably never be as versed in social media marketing, as someone is who devotes their entire career towards that topic. Likewise, a field as fluid as search engine optimization will likely be better covered by an SEO expert whose core focus is search engine optimization.

The T-Shaped Marketer

What this means for SMBs is that there's a fundamental choice each organization has to make with regard who manages their marketing. The answer to this question has to be based on the expertise and the skill set of your team, along with your budgetary constraints.

A vitally important question that has to be answered as quickly as possible is this: Can we, or should we, execute our digital marketing campaign in-house, utilize outside resources, or have a mix of both? Without a confirmed plan, your entire marketing focus could be slowed down without the right people or the right resources in place.

If your organization has people within their selected skill sets who have an interest in digital marketing or maybe even a background in marketing, it's important to ask the right questions to identify whether or not they might be a good fit for digital marketing. The digital marketer has at least six major qualities that are necessary to be a good fit for the role. These qualities include:

1. Have an analytical sense.

2. Are very well rounded.

3. Are perseverant.

4. Are disciplined.

5. Enjoy constant improvement and evolution.

6. Can manage adversity.

These questions will help you identify potential candidates for digital marketing. Whether it's the business owner or the most junior member of your team, these qualities are exceptionally important for successful digital marketers.

As we've talked about, digital marketing is a dynamically changing and rapidly growing part of any business. Having the wrong person involved within your digital marketing team can lead to a lack of success and a great deal of frustration.

In addition, this is not an area of business that is typically defined by a clear roadmap. A digital marketer has to be able to not only have a pragmatic approach to all things marketing, but they also have to be extremely creative.

This begets the question of whether a left-brain or right-brain individual is a better fit for digital marketing. It's my opinion that the rare person who is nearly identical left- and right-brain is typically the best fit in this position, especially for the SMB where the marketing team must wear many hats. That's not to say that an analytical or a creative person can't be a successful digital marketer. But for a small and medium-sized business organization that typically requires team members to manage multiple areas within digital marketing, there's a need for those who are both creative and numbers driven.

Always Follow the Data

One of the great benefits of digital marketing is the ability of the business owner to keep score and to measure the impact made on the organization's bottom line. Before the availability of digital marketing tracking and metrics, a frustrating element was the inability to measure much of what was created or produced. Business owners often gauged their success primarily by the bottom line success of the organization, which was also impacted by nearly every other business unit within the organization.

With the help of digital, marketing has gone from being a complementary segment of a company to a primary driver of the business. It's gone from being a supporting part to having a starring role.

Digital marketing has become an essential component of any sales and marketing program to the point that all businesses have to use digital channels to find prospects, turn them into leads, and then convert them into customers. If they don't, their competition will.

Having the ability to measure everything from a click in an email, to the time a lead spends on your website, to the source of where a lead has come from, allows the marketer to utilize this data to calibrate a highly defined and highly effective program. Knowing what is working and what doesn't not only makes for much more effective marketing but can also allow small and medium-sized businesses to grow the efficiency of their marketing programs and their return on investment.

Since every activity and interaction is now trackable, nearly every component of your digital marketing program should be constantly tested and its performance improved. Testing is a fundamental marketing tactic that allows you to optimize everything you manage.

For example, within email marketing, we can test multiple subject lines, changes in copy, images, and even when the messages are sent. We'll send these tests to a smaller segment of the mailing list, which will then give feedback on which version should sent to the rest of the list to be most effective.

This test-first methodology will exist across all of your digital marketing channels. You'll use similar testing techniques within paid digital advertising, search engine optimization, and social media as you will use within email marketing.

And the great part of all this is that these failure/success metrics are quickly and easily available. You can conduct multiple tests within a day, which would often take weeks with other traditional marketing channels that have a much longer execution cycle.

One of the hardest and most humbling aspects of digital marketing is the fact that testing nearly always wins over experience. You may think you know your market and your audience, but you most likely don't know how they'll react when they visit your site. That's why testing is vitally essential.

Yes, there are certain agreed upon rules that all landing pages must follow, such as limiting navigation, isolating on just a single offer, and keeping your primary call to action above the fold. However, beyond a few simple truths, what works for you must be developed by trial and error.

To prove that point, check out a website called "Anne Holland's Which Test Won – A/B Test & Multivariate Testing Education for Marketing Professionals" (it's at whichtestwon.com). The site shows you two different versions of a single landing page with subtle differences in the copy, images or layout. You select which page you believe had the better conversion percentage; after you "vote," you see the results. You'll almost always be surprised by the outcome.

The importance of testing and optimization means that any organization that employs a hypothesis or guess within their digital marketing is not properly utilizing the power of this technology. Because the data on what works or what doesn't work is readily available, there should never be guesses for any component of digital marketing.

Ignoring this information and going with an outside opinion, without testing those opinions, is not an effective strategy. Yes, there can be certain circumstances where you may create a campaign or program that provides solid results, but it could damage the brand itself. For example, if you created a provocative or racy banner ad that produced a fifteen percent click through rate, that campaign may be effective in the short term, but it could harm the brand in the long term and may not produce conversions into sales. To ignore data as your primary decision resource is to take a big gamble.

Organization and Time Management

With such a diverse breadth and depth of skills and expertise required, the role of a digital marketer could be compared to a plate spinner whose objective is to keep multiple plates balanced in the air without letting them drop. The skills and information required to become world-class in any one of area of digital marketing is a major challenge, let alone eight areas. However, someone has to be able to keep all of these plates in the air.

The key to managing a digital marketing program within a small and medium-sized business is to create a systematized approach. Keeping things organized and creating processes so that each of these various components is effectively conducted the way a small team or even a single person can manage digital marketing and get the most impactful, optimized programs.

Time, or a lack of it, is often the greatest challenge within digital marketing. Learning new skills, testing new approaches, and staying up-to-date on all of the changes present a consistent challenge for digital marketers. Whether you're working as a one-person sole proprietor or within a marketing department with hundreds of people, you have to be able to manage each aspect of your marketing. That typically means creating a process to deal with each marketing channel so it's constantly optimized and providing the most bang for the buck.

Having a time management process will allow you and your team to effectively use limited resources in the areas that are most appropriate. Spending time on marketing components that produce lesser impact will cause your organization and its performance to see diminished results.

It's a good idea to create an optimization task schedule that allows a digital marketer or digital marketing team to successfully and accurately allocate time and resources to each of the various components. Knowing what is happening when, and what needs to change, will often dictate how you spend your time.

However, as with all organizations, unexpected challenges will pop up on a fairly consistent basis. Having the flexibility to deal with these challenges while still helping the marketing group meet its goals is essential.

When assembled properly, all of your digital marketing channels should complement one another. In addition, these channels should complement your off-line channels. Your email marketing should complement your display advertising. Your social media marketing should complement your event marketing. That's why it's essential for a digital marketing campaign to include all digital and off-line components so that they can assist one another in managing the customer journey of each lead and help the organization develop and manage its business.

One major component of this that we'll discuss in a future section is building paths or email workflow tracks to assist your customer on their journey. This proactive approach of assisting your customer while utilizing your expertise to provide them with a clear roadmap is a key feature of some of the marketing automation tools now available within digital marketing. The parts of the customer relationship that were exclusively managed by a face-to-face or verbal dialogue are now often enhanced within the digital realm.

If the key asset within your organization is your expertise, then your challenge is to provide that expertise across the entire length of the customer buying cycle. What this means is there can be a significant amount of knowledge transfer before someone even becomes a lead.

This is extremely important for digital marketing where knowledge transfer and thought leadership are key indicators of success. Taking the approach of helping people solve their problems by utilizing your expertise will be a key strategy as we take a deeper look into the individual components of your digital marketing programs.

Chapter 2

Digital Platforms

Digital marketing platforms refer to the places that you can post your content or otherwise communicate with current or potential customers such as websites, e-mail, apps and social networks. The linchpin of most small and medium-sized business marketing platforms has traditionally been a website, primarily because it is the one platform that you exclusively own or control.

Along with the website, however, there are additional platforms such as social media sites. You also can have a mobile platform that you may run through an app or through your website as well. In addition, you can also use SMS text messaging to reach customers through their mobile devices.

According to a 2013 survey by marketing company Yodle, many small business owners have not yet adopted many digital marketing platforms. More than half of SMB owners do not have a website (52 percent) or even measure the results of their marketing programs (56 percent). This is a strong reminder that many small and medium-sized businesses need to take advantage of the available digital marketing channels and the audiences they attract.

Despite all of these different channels, the website is still the primary platform that nearly all businesses—especially small and medium-sized—use as the hub of their digital programs. Your website will act as the clearinghouse for the majority of your content and will typically be the centerpiece for your marketing campaigns.

In addition to the website, most SMBs will want to have a presence on social media channels that may be relevant to their company and to their audience. These social media channels provide a ready-made audience with which you can interact and become part of the community.

"Rent to Own" Platforms

What's important to understand is that the audience found on most social media platforms is basically "rent to own." For example, a network such as Facebook owns their platform and even owns the presence that you have created on that platform. If Facebook decides to remove your page, it is completely within their rights to do so, taking away the potential for a relationship with anyone on their platform (unless you buy advertising).

Therefore it's important to be aware of the "rent to own" structure of all social media channels. This means that a major goal when dealing with social media should be to convert your audience on that specific channel over to *your* website, so you can have more control over that relationship.

Mobile and SMS

Mobile marketing and mobile apps are another channel or platform in which you can have an ongoing dialogue with a current or potential customer. With smart phones continually gaining a larger share of time spent online, it's important to have a mobile relationship or at least offer a mobile-ready resource for your customers.

One final channel with which you can communicate with your audience would be standard SMS text messaging. As with most marketing channels, text messaging is a permission-based dialogue with your audience. Even though it's not as popular a marketing option as some other channels, it does provide a valuable conduit to reach your customer and the ability to maintain or retain an ongoing relationship.

Website Development Options

When choosing how to build your website, there are a number of different options available depending upon on your needs, goals and resources.

Blog Platform

A simple approach is to use a blog platform such as Blogger or WordPress.com in which you can insert information about your company into their previously created templates. These platforms are used by individuals and businesses to create a quick and easy website presence, but they're usually not the go-to source for creating a branded web site for a business.

FOR THIS BONUS ONLINE CONTENT VISIT
walterlis.com/resources

Content Management System

One of the most popular resources at the moment for creating websites is to use a content management system such as WordPress, Joomla!, or Drupal. A content management system is basically a software system that is often created as an open source program; however, there are other content management systems that are privately built, which I'll discuss next.

WordPress, Joomla! and Drupal are robust, free content management systems that can be customized and built into your own look and feel by using themes which are pre-built that you can modify. A positive element of using a content management system, especially an open source content management system, is that you have the power of thousands of people working together to build, manage, and improve the software.

That doesn't mean that these systems will be 100 percent foolproof and won't have some issues going forward. There can be various technical issues that you may come across when you're using this type of content management system. However the major platforms do offer a great deal of flexibility, and are typically not very difficult to install, customize, and manage for someone with moderate technical experience.

In 2014, nearly 22 percent of all websites were built using Wordpress, according to Web Technology Surveys. Wordpress owns a 60 percent share of the content management system market, followed by Joomla (9 percent) and Drupal (5 percent). Currently, 36 percent of all websites are built using a content management system.

In addition to open source CMS, there are also custom-built content management systems. A benefit to having a custom content management system is you can build it to fit within the framework of your organization and include the elements that you would like to have on your website. However, a downside to a customized content management system is when software changes, operating systems change or mobile platforms change, your content management system often has to be updated as well.

An additional decision could involve whether or not you want to take the steps to set up the open-source system or have a professional do it for you. Although most of these platforms are fairly easy to set up, they do require some technical knowledge. In my experience, they also will require some technical knowledge along the way as you manage your system and make changes to your platform.

FOR THIS BONUS ONLINE CONTENT VISIT
walterlis.com/resources

Themes and Plug-Ins

A major selling point for a content management system such as WordPress is the availability of thousands of pre-built themes that are available for purchase, some of which are also free. Also available are thousands of "plug-ins," which are applications that you can easily insert into your content management system to perform a specific task. These plug-ins allow you to do things such as add a contact form, custom calendar, or poll, or improve the search engine optimization of your website without having to know how to write code.

FOR THIS BONUS ONLINE CONTENT VISIT
walterlis.com/resources

Just be aware that adding these types of features, whether it be a custom theme or plug-in, increases the complexity of your WordPress installation, meaning you'll need to keep an eye on updates and potentially have some technical questions if you add a great deal of intricacies to your website. If you're not interested in using a content management system, there are other available options as well.

Nameplate Sites

Personal webpage or nameplate sites such as About.me, Flavors, and Vilify, are extremely quick ways to create a simple website. Typically these nameplate sites aggregate content that you provide and are very flexible. They can be a quick and easy way to get a presence online and can also be used to supplement your website and social media presence by adding another marketing channel and audience to help drive traffic to your website.

FOR THIS BONUS ONLINE CONTENT VISIT
walterlis.com/resources

Online Service

With an online service such as Weebly, you can select a template and add your own information. These services are somewhat similar to a blog platform such as WordPress.com, which is different than the content management system WordPress. This type of website online service is pretty much plug-and-play. You won't have complete control over the customization or flexibility, but it can be a significant upgrade from a personal webpage or nameplate site.

FOR THIS BONUS ONLINE CONTENT VISIT
walterlis.com/resources

Website Creation Software

You can build a website using a website creation tool or piece of software such as Dreamweaver. In the days before open source content management systems, a tool such as Dreamweaver was often a great way for a graphic designer to create a website without having a tremendous proficiency for coding. Dreamweaver provided an interface that allowed a graphic design to be imported and then would customize the coding and output flat files for the website.

**FOR THIS BONUS
ONLINE CONTENT VISIT**
walterlis.com/resources

Professional Website Developer

In addition to Dreamweaver, a final option to create a website would be to use a traditional website developer. This might be a good option for a larger organization that is looking to own every aspect of the design, along with the code for their website. Obviously, the downside is that these code options must be able to be customized and be added to so you can continue to add content to the website. Despite these hurdles, there still are some small and medium-sized businesses that choose to hire a developer to write the code for their new website.

Website Hosting

If you're using a content management system, or are building your own website, then another component that you'll need to plan for is web hosting. Because most small to medium-sized businesses aren't in the market to buy their own web server to host their own website, using a professional hosting company is a logical choice that can be both easy and cost effective.

Hosting companies typically charge a monthly or annual fee to host your website and conduct other additional services to make sure that your site is up and running. Good hosting companies also will help you deal with specific components of your website that may require service or updates.

**FOR THIS BONUS
ONLINE CONTENT VISIT**
walterlis.com/resources

A hosting company can also help you purchase a domain name to use for your website. Having the right domain name for your business is essential because you want to make it as easy as possible for people to find your website. Good domain names are easy to remember, easy to spell, easy to pronounce, and often short.

Storage Capacity and Memory

When looking for a web hosting company, an important element to consider is storage capacity. Having enough storage capacity to hold your website and plan for its future growth and future traffic is essential. You might want to add audio files, video, and images to your website, which can often use up storage capacity. Having the right amount of disk space is definitely an important consideration.

Another important element when choosing a web host is memory. Be sure to find a web host that will offer sufficient memory, along with CPU or processing power to make sure that your applications are running efficiently. Without enough memory and without proper power, some local applications that you have on your website, such as video, can perform poorly and affect the user's experience.

It's important to realize that a new visitor to a website tends to be impatient. If a website is slow or if a page is slow to load, studies have shown that the visitor will often leave within a matter of seconds. According to a report in *The New York Times*, a visitor will visit a website less often if it is slower than that of a close competitor by more than 250 milliseconds (a millisecond is a thousandth of a second).

For websites that are using a content management system or being built with a database, you'll need to have access to a large enough database to manage your applications. For most content management systems, the database will interface directly with the content management system and is typically managed without a large degree of complexity.

Something else to consider when purchasing web hosting is the fact that your employees' email accounts will often be a part of your hosting package, especially for small and medium-sized businesses. Therefore it's important to identify how many email accounts you can create and how large those email accounts can be. A number of solid web hosts now offer unlimited email accounts.

Server Types

Another choice you'll have with regard to web hosting will be what type of server works best for your organization. There are typically three different types of servers: shared servers, dedicated servers, and virtual servers.

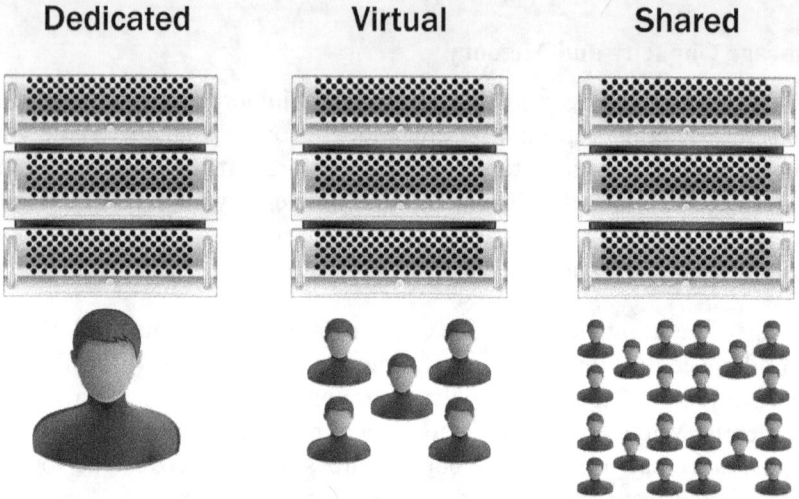

| Dedicated | Virtual | Shared |

A **shared server** is just as the name alludes to, a server that is shared amongst multiple clients. The upside with a shared server is the cost is usually much lower than a dedicated or virtual server. The downside with a shared server is your bandwidth and speed can be affected by other websites that are hosted on your shared server.

In addition, if you are using that server with the same IP address to host your employees' email accounts, you could have another concern. If that server is blacklisted because other clients on your shared server have been sending spam email, you could also have issues as well when trying to send email.

The other option is a **dedicated server**, which basically means you would own a server or at least access to your own server. Having a dedicated server means you are probably going to pay more because you're the only person who will be using that server. However, it precludes you from having to deal with other companies' websites and their potential headaches. A dedicated server can also provide a certain level of peace of mind because you will be the only organization who owns access to that server.

A **virtual server** is a hybrid version of a shared and dedicated server. A virtual server uses a partition to split the server into multiple components. Virtual servers offer a higher level of security and protection from other organizations using that server, and they also provide a lower price point, typically because multiple organizations are able to share the horsepower on that server. Be sure to talk with each hosting company to decide whether a shared, dedicated or virtual server would work best for you.

Since servers are computers, they need an operating system to manage their needs. The two primary operating systems for servers are Windows servers, and Linux servers. Most WordPress installations prefer a Linux-based server, while Windows servers manage a majority of other applications.

Other final thoughts on web hosting include some items that you'll want to discuss with your hosting company. Some hosting companies offer unlimited bandwidth claims, which can often include caveats attached. Be sure to check with the hosting company and have them explain exactly what they mean by "unlimited bandwidth."

Most hosting companies with a solid reputation will offer 24/7 customer service and support. In addition, they will offer support for outside applications within the hosting environment. Top-level hosts will often provide some assistance when dealing with a content management system.

This is extremely important, because if you're looking to make changes to your website and don't understand why something is happening, it's important to have an expert to help you sort things out, especially during the off hours. As you work to turn your website into a lead machine, it becomes extremely important that this lead machine does not stop running for a significant period of time.

Chapter 3

Search Engine Optimization

For the majority of small and medium-sized businesses, a large amount of traffic that you'll receive on your website and other online channels will often come from search engines. The majority of this traffic will come from Google, which is the leader among search engines by a wide margin. That's not to say that Bing or Yahoo searches aren't worth the time, but studies have shown that the lion's share of search traffic will come from Google.

What is search engine optimization? I think a better question is, "What is optimization as it relates to search engines?" What it *isn't* is search engine marketing. That term is often used along with search engine optimization as though the two are interchangeable. However, in my opinion, there is no such thing as search engine marketing.

In reality, the search engines are the owners of the audience that uses their website to search the Internet. It's basically their decision to send traffic to your website, meaning that there is little or no marketing involved as it relates to search engines, unless you're buying advertising.

What is available, however, is working with search engines to provide their visitors the best search possible. What that means is you must identify what the main goal or purpose is for a search engine.

According to Google (www.google.com/about/company/philosophy), their primary goal is to provide the most relevant authoritative search results to assist their audience. Meaning, if I search for a particular search term, I can expect Google to provide me with the highest quality information possible regarding that search term.

Therefore it's essential to understand what Google is trying to accomplish. Marketers sometimes look at Google as being a competitor, or a riddle that they need to decode. Trying to reverse engineer the search algorithm has been a quest that many have tried in vain to accomplish.

But the proper tactic, and more importantly, the proper mindset, should be to think of Google, Yahoo, and Bing as your search partners. That obviously goes against much of what is written within search engine optimization discussion; however since this is not yet your audience, your best bet is to learn how to play by the proper rules and give the search engines exactly what they need to be successful with their job.

So if Google's purpose is to provide the most relevant articles and the best results on each search for each consumer, then it's *your* job to give Google whatever it needs so that your information and your expertise is available to them. That doesn't mean you will be creating content and writing articles specifically for Google. But it does mean that you'll be aware of the specific priorities and recommendations that Google makes so they can access your articles and information quickly and efficiently. Then when a search engine crawls your site, your content can appear for the appropriate search query in their search results.

Here's another extremely important point. Search engines, and the algorithms that they use to help convert a search query into search results, are always changing.

Google search engine algorithms literally change every day. What that means is trying to create content or modify your website to reverse engineer a Google algorithm is a losing battle. A better approach is to find out what Google is looking for *in general*, and give them exactly what they need.

So what are Google and other search engines looking for? What are the points that they, as a business, need to make sure that customers continue to come back to Google, and not defect to another search engine? Here are some of the top recommended components that Google has shared with us over the years.

What Google Wants

Google looks for highly relevant, unique, quality, original content. First and foremost, your articles have to be new, and they have to be original. With the technology available to the search engines these days, copying someone else's work is quickly and easily revealed. Therefore you need to be able to provide your own voice and your own expertise in your own unique and engaging way.

Whenever possible, it's also a great idea to take a deep dive into particular subjects and topics that are within your expertise. The more in-depth information that you can provide within your range of knowledge, the better chance you'll have of being unique and standing out amongst all the other potential information providers.

Another component that is essential for search engines is the concept of authority. If I'm searching for a particular question, I not only want to have in-depth, quality information, but would prefer that it come from a highly knowledgeable and trusted source. Google realizes this and favors content providers with a larger degree of authority within their search engine algorithm. Therefore, if an expert financial analyst writes an article about managing investments, their specific topic authority will have a much better chance of ranking high in the search engine output than someone with no background in finance who writes on that topic.

Identifying this authority by search engines is dictated by a number of factors. Two primary factors are *back links* from other websites to that particular article and the *social authority* of that author. This could include Facebook likes, re-Tweets, or any other sharing of links towards this content or by showing signs of approval across other social media networks.

The topic of whether social signals impact search engine rankings has been debated for many years. Google itself has provided mixed messages on this issue. However, I agree with Neil Patel's take and the importance of social media on SEO from this excellent article – (www.quicksprout.com/2014/04/11/why-social-is-the-new-seo).

In any case, if you write a well thought-out and highly researched, valuable article about a specific topic and are successful in sharing that content with a large audience, two things may happen.

1. There's a good chance many of your readers will *link to* your article from their websites and blogs.

2. Your readers may also *share* your article with friends across all their social networks.

When this happens the search engines are able to collect this data and determine that due to these factors, there is a very good chance you know what you're talking about. When that takes place, your article will often appear closer to the top of search engine results for relevant keywords.

So how can a small and medium-sized business improve their authority beyond just creating good quality content and participating in social media channels? One targeted way to improve your chances to draw interest in your content and attract backlinks from other websites is to create specific content based upon a key search term or phrase.

Linkable Assets

An in-depth report, top ten list, or expert interview are all examples of a term called "linkable assets." What we mean by "linkable assets" are high quality, well researched, and well thought-out pieces of content that provide so much value that other websites or online sources will refer their circle of influence to your work. This is a win-win situation because the searcher is finding exactly what they need with your in-depth content, and you, the content creator, will receive the votes of authority that allow your material to improve in the eyes of the search engines.

It's important to consider, however, that writing and creating these linkable assets can be a significant investment of time and resources. Therefore it's essential to identify the best topics about which you'll be creating content before you start this process.

**FOR THIS BONUS
ONLINE CONTENT VISIT**
walterlis.com/resources

Before creating linkable assets, I recommend that you do a significant amount of research to see what's attracting interest and traffic within your industry and what might be worth adding your expertise. There are a number of **SEO tools available** that can help you identify what's a hot topic before you go down the path of creating your best work.

**FOR THIS BONUS
ONLINE CONTENT VISIT**
walterlis.com/resources

Website Structure and Google Results

There are additional factors outside of your content that can play a significant role in your search engine optimization efforts. One of these factors relates to the internal and external structure of your website.

If your site provides a quick and efficient return based on a query or link by showing your pages quickly, you'll have a better chance of keeping an audience on your website. This *website speed* or *page load time* is essential to Google because searchers typically have very short attention spans and an even shorter amount of patience when waiting for search results. What that means is your website has to be fast and efficient.

Factors that dictate website speed are both internal and external. Having a solid website host with significant bandwidth and a fast database can help speed the process. If you have a website that calls a number of search queries within the code and utilizes complex algorithms, content management system plug-ins, or other devices that can tax your server's bandwidth, key pages on your website could be slow and lethargic.

Speed is essential, and providing customers with rapid results should be an extremely high priority for your website. To help in identifying items that could be slowing down your processing, Google and others provide **online webmaster tools** that will query your website and provide suggestions on how to improve your response times. You can get started at google.com/webmasters/.

**FOR THIS BONUS
ONLINE CONTENT VISIT**
walterlis.com/resources

Another important factor that Google has recommended is providing a quality experience for visitors to your website no matter what type of device that they're using. If I'm searching on a mobile device such as a phone or tablet, and your website forces me to manipulate my screen just to read your content, I'll probably not be happy with that experience, especially on a smaller screen. Therefore Google has recommended that all websites have the ability to flexibly present their content so that users of all devices can quickly and easily access their information.

This may have been a challenge a couple years ago, but with the advent of responsive design, this is now a manageable issue. The concept of responsive design is taking the components of a website and producing it in such a way that the information can be dynamically generated in a legible and easy to read format no matter what platform or device you may be using.

Having a mobile-ready website is imperative for search engines so that they can continue to provide their searchers the best possible experience. Whether you use a responsive design website or you create a mobile-only site is up to you. But be advised that having a one-size-fits-all website that doesn't work well with mobile will almost certainly be looked on as a negative by the search engines.

Make Your Website Crawlable

After you complete all of the previously mentioned recommendations from the search engines, the most important factor for allowing the search engines to get your information is to make them "crawlable." Google has what they term "spiders" or "Googlebots" that search the Internet for information. If your website is accessible, the Googlebot will visit your site and catalog your content so they can present your expertise to their searchers.

The important part to note here is that you need to be sure to allow your website to be crawled. If you're using a content management system, a common error is to build your website in a non-crawlable state and keep it restricted from the Googlebot, even after your website has launched. This will prohibit Google from crawling your site and will keep you from ranking for any of your relevant search terms.

**FOR THIS BONUS
ONLINE CONTENT VISIT**
walterlis.com/resources

Using **webmaster tools**, whether from Google, Bing or others will help you identify how many web pages have been crawled on your website, and how often they have been accessed by the search engines. I highly recommend that you bookmark and visit these sites often so you can determine what may or may not need to be changed on your website, or if you're making any basic errors that may be prohibiting the search engines from crawling your site.

Visitor Friendliness

In addition to all the factors that we've already discussed that allow the search engines access to your website, another important factor is the usability of your website for actual human beings. Following traditional link structure methods that allow people to logically access information on your website in a simple and straightforward format is essential. This may seem as though it is an obvious component of building a website, but it can be easily overlooked depending upon the vision of the developer or if you are trying to accomplish too much with a particular page or layout.

Always be aware of how difficult it may be for someone to find what they're searching for on your website. It's a great idea to have someone who knows absolutely nothing about your product or service to visit your website and asked them to perform a variety of searches to find particular pieces of information. If they struggle or can't identify how to find things, this is a good indicator that you'll need to reassess your page structure and your layout.

Another important factor within search engine optimization is the prevalence of mobile search by consumers. Search queries are now, and will continue to become, more popular on mobile devices. What this means for the search engine is an increasing need for fluid results based upon the user's preferences and/or their geographic or demographic information. What this means for you as a content producer is the importance of providing as much information within the content and within the code on your website. Using suggested markup languages, such as the

Schema.org and Facebook Open Graph protocol can go a long way in accomplishing this.

In addition to mobile search, voice search is growing in popularity. Consumers are now often speaking their search queries instead of typing. The impact of this is that searchers often will speak a different structure of search than they may type. This once again points to the importance of having your content tagged properly so search engines can find it.

Google offers a service called "search assist." Search assist occurs when you start typing a particular word or set of words into their search bar and you're immediately presented with a number of suggestions. This service occurs only if you have the search assist turned on, but it too can have a big impact on search engine rankings as the search engines can theoretically steer a query in one direction or another with their ideas.

A good practice is to test the keywords or phrases that your business is looking to rank for within the search bar and see what similar phrases are produced by search assist. You can then use these additional keywords and phrases within your content so that you can be involved in some more of these searches.

Chapter 4

Content Marketing

The term "content marketing" could be considered somewhat repetitive because practically all marketing involves content. In reality, content marketing or "inbound marketing" has been around for over a century in one form or another, practiced by all kinds of businesses.

Using content for marketing is the practice of creating relevant and compelling information to help share an organization's expertise. Back in 1895, the John Deere Company created *The Furrow*, which was one of the first corporate newsletters or magazines. The premise of the magazine was to help farmers to better utilize John Deere equipment and improve the profitability of the farm. Since that time, many companies of all sizes around the world have used a corporate newsletter magazine or other marketing channel to help educate their clients and keep their customer relationships intact.

So why is content marketing so popular now, since it's been around for so long? Well, the first reason is that if you're not producing content in the digital era, you'll be drowned out by your competition. It's that simple. The audience is there and your competitors are probably there; and if they're not, they will be. In today's information age, content is king.

Another reason for the surge in content is that the infrastructure of traditional media has changed drastically, especially in the twenty-first century with the advent of social media and other digital channels. What used to take a newspaper or mass media focused organization can now be accomplished through this network of information "pipes" that brings content from any one of us to all of us. In reality, all companies are now media companies.

The first step of all business relationships is sharing some form of expertise. Whether you're visiting a bricks-and-mortar store, speaking over the phone, or communicating via email, a customer will reach out to a company for information relevant to their needs. In today's digital world, it's now your job to be one step ahead and *reach out* to your potential customers with helpful information around your expertise.

So just what are we talking about in terms of types of content marketing? What types of informational content could you create? Here are a few examples:

Blog posts, how-to guides, images, infographics, video, illustrations, testimonials, case studies, webinars, email newsletters, e-books, podcasts, quizzes, games, apps, interactive demos, press releases, case studies, checklists, reviews, and ratings.

How is information content used?

All businesses need to create content for each stage of the customer relationship. The four stages that I'll discuss are demand generation, lead generation, lead nurturing, and customer evangelists.

Connecting the right types of content with these four different stages of where a customer could be in their relationship is at the core of digital marketing. Your expertise is to link your customers to the appropriate channel.

What, then, should you create?

When approaching content creation it's imperative to take a pragmatic approach to identify which itch needs to get scratched. What I mean by this is there is no reason to guess what your audience may want.

Obviously your expertise and history helping your customers will be your best guide, but that doesn't necessarily mean that creating content that answers their questions will automatically be the right path. Secondly, there are data and specific tools that can help identify possible targets. A perfect mix is often a balance of experience and data.

Tools For Search Results Research

So how can you identify the biggest itch in your industry? Firstly, there are tools that provide services, such as *backlink analysis,* that allow you to find out what other websites are pointing towards as well as the most popular articles in your industry.

FOR THIS BONUS ONLINE CONTENT VISIT
walterlis.com/resources

For example, if one of your competitors creates a how-to list about assembling a specific product, and you see that there are number of other websites pointing to that piece of content, that gives you a good idea that your competitor's how-to list worked. You can get this type of information on virtually any topic online.

Another tool that is very helpful in this area is Google Trends. This free product provides you with examples of what's being searched for and what's gaining popularity on Google. This is an excellent tool that can give you lots of ideas on potential topics to investigate.

Another valuable content research tool is using the search assist function in Google. This simply occurs when you start to type something into the Google search bar and additional words or search phrases are presented as you begin to type. (Note that you must have this feature turned on in order to get the Google auto-complete suggestions.) This is another great way to find out what the popular search terms that are related to what you're writing about.

And finally, a fourth way to identify potential topics for content is to use paid search advertising tools. AdWords is a paid search ad platform from Google that also comes with several tools that allow you to see the size of a marketplace as well as how many searches are being requested for specific keywords.

Assembling a list of keywords and analyzing what their opportunity could be is the first step to providing a framework when deciding what you could potentially create content about. The second step is identifying how much competition there is for a particular keyword. This capability is also available through numerous *keyword analysis and marketing tools* as well as within Google AdWords.

**FOR THIS BONUS
ONLINE CONTENT VISIT**
walterlis.com/resources

Granted, if there are specific keywords that are highly competitive and they are in the middle of your organization's sweet spot, then you still will probably consider writing content or creating content for that keyword. However it's always a good idea to know what you might be up against before you begin.

Your Customer Persona

Once you have some topic ideas, your target becomes identifying your exact audience. Since your company is the expert, you'll have a good idea of whom you will be writing for. However, it's essential to create what are called a "customer persona" before you begin.

Example Customer Personas

Jennifer - 36 Years Old
Married - 2 Kids
Graphic Designer
Loves NPR
Practices Yoga

David - 28 Years Old
Single
Accountant
Loves Action Movies
Plays Basketball

When I started writing this book, I identified my audience as key stakeholders for small and medium-sized businesses. Every page that I wrote and every topic that I researched, I thought in terms of what my audience would want or need. I had a very clear vision of their key characteristics, which helped me to refine the various aspects of each topic that was covered.

41

A customer persona is a vivid identification with as many key parts as possible of your targeted customer. You could have one or multiple customer personas that you're looking to target. The best customer personas have the most information and are able to create the most vivid realization of that customer.

You'll want to consider coming up with a name for that persona to aid your recollection. You may even want to create an illustration or photo for display while you're creating the content so you're often reminded of whom you're writing for.

Lead Magnets

Once you've identified whom you're targeting and what the potential types of content are, your next challenge is to identify what we call *"lead magnets"* to help attract leads to your website. A lead magnet is a piece of content with enough value that a consumer would be willing to trade a piece of their contact information, such as an email address, for it. Building a lead list by using your digital channels and using lead magnets is a great way to exchange value for value.

How to Create Quality Content

We've talked about a lot of different types of content and different routes to take in order to create that content. The elephant in the room right now is how are we going to do this? There is no getting around the fact that creating good quality content takes time and resources.

One technique that helps marketers utilize their resources in the best manner is taking a strategic approach towards content creation. An example of this is to create one piece of content and transform it into many different formats.

For example, you could record a video interview, which would then be turned into an audio podcast, which would then be transcribed into text, then turned into a blog post, and subsequently turned into an infographic. One simple interview is leveraged into multiple pieces of content, maximizing the value while minimizing the costs and resources required.

A good strategy to take when creating content is to emphasize quality over quantity. Search engines have historically rewarded sites that consistently create valuable content. I've found that very good quality content will typically attract more content and more leads over the long haul versus a larger number of less valuable articles or blog posts.

Since there is a lot of potential work in this realm, it's important to involve the various stakeholders and thought leadership experts within your organization to help with this task. Remember, your company and all companies are media channels, meaning everyone needs to be involved.

It's also important for customers to understand the true value that your organization can provide. Limiting customer exposure to just a few key individuals could also limit the potential value and expertise they see in your organization.

One very helpful tool to use when creating content is an ***editorial calendar***. You can create a simple calendar or you can use one of the many readily available plug-ins for your content management system to identify and create content as well as plan for its release.

FOR THIS BONUS ONLINE CONTENT VISIT
walterlis.com/resources

I'm a big believer in creating a strategy and doing your research so that managing the content and building the content is much more manageable in the future. You might think that after all of this research and effort, and once your various content marketing pieces are created, your job will be complete—but this is often just the beginning. I'll soon reveal the various ways that you'll want to promote this content including email marketing, social sharing, social groups, and guest posting.

Chapter 5

Email Marketing

Despite the advent of numerous new marketing channels and opportunities, email marketing is often still a preferred method of communication for most business relationships. Consumers prefer email because it is typically less intrusive than a phone call and the dialog can be controlled fairly easily through an email client. In addition, email is flexible, customizable, and won't be lost or go away, as opposed to the immediacy of the phone call.

From a marketer's perspective or from a small and medium-sized business perspective, email is highly cost effective, as compared to other types of direct mail or similar one-to-one correspondence. Whether you send your emails through your own email system, or you're using an email provider, which is probably the preferred method, it's hard to beat the cost of email.

Another benefit of email is that it's easily trackable. Using an *email provider*, or even an analytics program such as Google Analytics, you can track numerous essential email marketing metrics. How many people are opening your email? How many of your emails bounced or were not received? How many people have forwarded your email? How many people have clicked on your email? These are examples of important metrics for you to track and to gauge the response of your email marketing.

**FOR THIS BONUS
ONLINE CONTENT VISIT**
walterlis.com/resources

With these metrics comes the ability to test email marketing with an efficiency unlike any other one-to-one marketing correspondence. If you're sending direct snail mail, testing requires time. The steps required include: create and send a direct mail piece, wait days for the results, and then adjust the creative. With email marketing, you receive campaign results instantly, allowing you to make decisions and adjustments on the fly and without the need for additional resources.

The key driver to success using email marketing is *relevancy*, which means providing the right message to the audience that's looking for it. Your goal when sending email is to target either a person, or a persona, and give them information that they've requested or could use. This will help eliminate unnecessary emails, and improve your overall relationship with your customers and potential customers.

One major positive aspect for email and the response it generates has been the CAN-SPAM Act. The CAN-SPAM Act was signed into law in December of 2003 and established the United States' first national standards for the sending of commercial email. Its primary goal was to help consumers protect their privacy and create an element of trust that was missing at the time between the email senders and receivers. Consumers can now be much more confident that if they want to remove themselves from an email list they can do so quickly and easily.

Despite advances in confidence and relevancy of messaging, in quarter two of 2013, the percentage of spam in total email increased by 4.2 percent over the first quarter and came to 70.7 percent. Allowing your email to have the best opportunity to reach your audience means it must go above and beyond ordinary means to overcome the negative effects that spam creates.

For email marketing, the ultimate goal is to build your relationship with your customer or potential customer by using the "know-like-trust" factor. Your initial emails should be created in such a way that they provide valuable, relatable content so the reader can identify immediate value, and they know you. As they continue to receive these emails that help them and assist in their needs, your relationship will advance into the like stage. String together enough solid communications and provide enough good assistance for your customers and you have a shot at reaching the pinnacle, which is a trusting relationship.

Types of Emails

When creating emails, there are two primary targets. You have emails for either an individual person or one of your marketing personas. Knowing for whom you are creating the email is essential, and it is something that you must consistently remind yourself of when you're in your planning or development stages.

The most popular type of email campaign is identified as a *direct response email*, which is created for an individual person. A direct response email is helpful when you have some basic information about a person with whom you've been in contact previously and now can provide a much more directed response message.

A *lead nurturing email* is part of a series of emails or workflow that is crafted to maximize the know-like-trust factor. Lead nurturing emails are highly strategic in nature and consist of multiple emails that replicate real-world relationships through the use of automated email marketing.

For example, say a potential customer provides you their email address after downloading a whitepaper report on your website You'll probably want to include this person in a lead nurturing email campaign that immediately starts by providing valuable information surrounding the product that they've shown interest in and gives them additional information based on your expertise. As you continue to send lead nurturing emails over a period of time, you'll advance the relationship, working to earn trust with your potential customer.

One of the great components of lead nurturing through automated email campaigns is the ability to enhance relationships without the need for extra time or resources. If you do your job right, you'll be able to provide your sales team with warm leads who know, like, and trust you, your company, and your products.

A final type of email is a *broadcast email*, which typically would be considered something like an email newsletter. Although these may be more generalized in nature, your newsletter should still be sent to a segmented portion of your email list depending upon their interests. It's in your best interest to send highly targeted campaigns with a focused message to the most relevant portions of your email list. One size does not fit all in the world of email marketing, because a message that does not resonate won't be opened and read; or even worse, it might be considered spam.

Crafting Your Message

Email marketing is part science and part art. A few crucial aspects of email marketing can dictate your success and failure. Creating emails is something that nearly everyone does, but creating successful email marketing requires a great deal of skill and expertise.

When developing your messages, it's important to be brief and get to the point quickly. Forcing your reader to scroll through an extended message is a recipe for disaster. Emails that are easily digestible will attract a better response rate and have more people involved.

It's also important to always write for the mind of your reader. What I mean by this is to always think of what you can do to help your consumer first by providing value. If you can provide your customer with value, you'll typically have the opportunity to earn trust.

Another important aspect of successful email writing is to speak with a conversational tone that is relatable and shareable. Think about how you would write an email to a friend or family member and try to replicate that tone. Corporate business speak might be appropriate for a business plan or internal analysis, but email is an inherently one-on-one communication. Write like you speak and you'll have a much better chance appealing to a person, instead of a business plan.

In my opinion, your ability to write effectively might be the most essential and lucrative component of digital marketing. This is where the rubber meets the road; this is where you communicate directly with a lead. You cannot overestimate the impact that successful writing can have within your digital marketing. To this end, I strongly suggest that you look upon your copywriting as a never-ending skill set that has to be exercised, tested, and improved on a daily basis.

A great tool that most top email copywriters use is what's called a *swipe file*. A swipe file is essentially a collection of emails—subject lines, copy, calls to action, or basically any other component of an email that's worth saving. Having examples of great email messages can be extremely helpful when you're creating your own campaigns.

Email Acceptance by the Recipient

When you send an email to a friend or family member, you typically expect it to be opened and read. Most emails that are unwanted are not opened, whether it's from someone you may know or don't know. Therefore, it's extremely important to establish a basic level of awareness so you're recognized quickly.

If your potential customer knows you, and most preferably their primary point of contact within your organization, they will be much more incentivized to open up your message. If they're not familiar with you and the emails are coming from an organization that they don't know, the odds of them opening the email, despite your best efforts in writing a solid subject line, will be limited.

In a worst-case scenario, if you send out email that is unwanted, that email can be marked as spam and can hurt your reputation with your audience, as well as with email service providers. Damaging your standing with these two groups is akin to having a very negative public opinion.

With each email sent there are basically four potential options for its final destination. Emails will either be opened, ignored, unsubscribed, or listed as spam. Only one of those four choices is positive for your small and medium-sized business. Getting your emails opened is your primary concern and where any organization should focus first.

Email open rates are affected by the sender, which is the name of the organization sending email, and your email address. As mentioned previously, it's a good idea to have any email correspondence come from an individual person, so the reader can relate to a human being instead of an inanimate object. The best-case scenario is when your reader knows the person within your organization from whom they're receiving the email. This will always help open rates as that level of trust has already been established.

If the reader chooses to ignore your email, that could be either a temporary or permanent setback. It will be up to your next email, or additional work that you might do, to re-establish that relationship to help turn that ignore into an open.

Email that triggers an unsubscribe from your list is not necessarily a negative outcome. If someone receives what could be described as a relevant offer with valuable content and they don't feel as though that information is worth their time, then it's good for both parties if they are removed from your list. It's better to find out who might be a good match for your product as quickly as possible so you can focus your resources to better matches within your lead pool.

Obviously the worst case of the four email options is when a reader marks your message as spam. When a spam marking occurs, you've struck out on both the message and the audience.

Even more damaging is the potential that your reputation with Internet service providers and email hosting companies could be negatively affected. Your reputation amongst these gatekeepers is vitally important to allow your email to get through to their customers. If you send too many emails that trigger spam responses from an organization or email provider, you may have a hard time getting your messages through to those people who really want your communications and use those email platforms.

A good idea is to use a tool such as (mail-tester.com) that will test for spam triggers and provide you with a projected email deliverability score. This won't help a poor match of content and audience, but it will help you identify key words or phrases that email service providers typically mark as spam. It's essential to continually work to protect your email reputation so you can continue to have a consistent information exchange with your email list.

List Building

I like to use the analogy that the email address is the tinder to spark the fire process of becoming a lead. Generating a fire requires something to catch that spark in order to ignite. The email address is the most basic level of contact information that will allow you to reach out to a lead. Building a list of email addresses that is relevant to your products and services should be your primary goal.

There are many ways to approach building your email list so that you attract targets for your products and services. The primary way is to create great email content that people want to open. Approaching with the give-to-get mentality where you are providing your expertise, knowledge and information for free is always a useful tool in attracting potential leads and building your audience.

An additional way to build your email list is to create a *lead generation offer* or lead magnet, which I mentioned earlier. These are valuable information products that provide so much value for the right audience that potential customers are willing to exchange their contact information for the lead magnet.

Once again, this is a give-to-get scenario where you'll need to invest the time and resources up front to create something of great value, whether it's an ebook, resource guide, checklist, or any of a number of other options that readers or users consider worth exchanging their contact information for.

Hosting a **webinar** that allows your organization to demonstrate its expertise and help consumers is another great way to generate leads for your email list. In addition to the webinar, you can host an online contest to help build interest and your audience.

FOR THIS BONUS ONLINE CONTENT VISIT
walterlis.com/resources

You can also build your email list by including *calls to action* within your website. These calls to action are typically banner ads or text mentions within the context of your website that are linked to what's known as a landing page where you'll have an offer to exchange your lead magnet for customer contact information.

Another option is to partner with other complementary products or organizations to share your content within their marketing channels. For example, if you have content that could provide value to another organization, you could offer to share that lead magnet in exchange for the contacts that it might generate.

One other way to build your email list is to collect contact information in *offline environments*. If you attend conferences and trade shows within your industry, you can collect business cards or scan information to include in a direct response or lead nurturing campaign to help achieve the know, like, trust factor.

Landing Page Analysis

As mentioned earlier, the primary driver for successful email marketing is to provide the *right message* to the *right audience* at the *right time*. Miss out on any of these three variables and you'll often be met with resistance. Successfully navigate these three areas and you'll find a sweet spot and a powerful tool for your email communication.

A primary key to successful lead generation and email marketing is creating customized landing pages that you give your reader exactly what they expect, and make the next step in your relationship crystal clear. For example, if you have created an offer to download your lead magnet, you'll want to create a customized landing page on your website that will describe the offer, show the product, provide quick and easy description of the benefits of the content, and include a form for the consumer to exchange their contact information.

**FOR THIS BONUS
ONLINE CONTENT VISIT**
walterlis.com/resources

Landing pages, just as emails, need to be tested and optimized in order to improve their conversion rate and their effectiveness. This process of conversion rate optimization allows you to leverage the benefits of trackability and testing that most solid email marketing tools provide. As your landing pages receive traffic, you'll be able to analyze whether people respond to the offer in a positive manner. A landing page best practice is to have two versions of each page, with a single difference between each so you can see if it positively or negatively affects response rates.

Once you've identified which landing page version provides the best return, you'll remove the losing version, and create a new variation of the winning design. Then you'll make a subtle change to that new version and begin the test process again. This optimization strategy is a great way to truly leverage the power of digital marketing tools and the benefits that they can provide.

Optimizing your email marketing and your landing pages will not only improve your response rates, but it will enhance your return on investment. It's much cheaper to optimize and improve the conversion of the people who are already visiting your website than it is to attract new traffic to your website. Keep this in mind as you move forward with the rest of your digital marketing plans.

Chapter 6

Digital Advertising

The world of digital advertising has changed drastically over the past few years. The options available and the ability to track, test, and improve responses have definitely enhanced the opportunity for advertisers to reach their target audience using digital channels.

Guitar Lessons - MyMusic**Lessons**.co    ⓘ
`Ad` www.mymusic**lessons**.co/ ▾ (855) 438-5377
Teachers with college degrees great with kids, lots of references

Guitar Lessons (Videos) - JamPlay.com
`Ad` www.jamplay.com/**Guitar-Lessons** ▾ 4 8 ★ ★ ★ ★ ★ advertiser rating
3,500+ HD **Guitar Lessons** from Pros. Join 250K Guitarists on JamPlay!
Tour of JamPlay - JamPlay Free Trial - 68 Teachers - Learn A Style

Guitar Lessons - Free Online **Guitar Lessons** for Beginners
www.**guitarlessons**.com/ ▾
Welcome to **GuitarLessons**.com. This is a free resource for guitarists that are interested
in expanding their musical abilities. It's the ultimate source of free online ...
Online Guitar Lessons - Beginner Guitar Quick-Start - Guitar Chords - Jam Tracks

Stonegrove **Guitar** - Private Music **Lessons** and Repair
stonegrove**guitar**.com/ ▾
Essential Information. Stonegrove **Guitar** 721 W. Hillgrove Ave. LaGrange, IL 60525 (708)
588-0777. Email Us · Directions. HOURS: Mon-Thurs: 12-8pm. Fri-Sat:

Sponsored search is a primary digital advertising channel that typically draws the lion's share of revenue for search providers such as Google and

Bing. Sponsored search ads are promotions that appear next to the organic results for a relevant keyword search phrase. For example, if you wanted to advertise your product that is a lawnmower, you would create a sponsored search ad listing, choose your keyword ("lawnmower"), and put a bid in for that ad. Subsequently, when someone searches for the term "lawnmower," your ad would be shown in the sponsored search results of the search engine.

**FOR THIS BONUS
ONLINE CONTENT VISIT**
walterlis.com/resources

Social media marketing has evolved into a powerhouse ***digital advertising platform***. Certainly the massive audiences that social media channels have attracted make an obvious target for advertisers wanting to bring their product or service to that audience. The second half of this equation is the fact that the social media channels themselves have become more creative in recent years in terms of ways an advertiser can bring their message to the audience of that social media channel. Sponsored stories, embedded messages, and other tactics are available in addition to traditional text or banner ads opportunities within nearly all social media networks.

Mobile marketing is a constantly changing environment due to the rapid influx and market acceptance of smart phones in the United States and globally. Savvy marketers have been able to leverage the power of SMS or text marketing to help start communication directly with their customers. As bandwidth has increased and the percentage of smart phone users has skyrocketed, mobile marketing has evolved into a solid platform to reach consumers while they are in action, which could be at a store, at an event, or even while they're riding the bus.

Email marketing has been a channel that has experienced its share of fluctuations in terms of efficiency and success. However, when strategically executed, with precise targeting and segmentation, the opportunity to enhance a relationship with a one-to-one conversation using email marketing can be a strong method to build and grow an audience. Advertising within emails can also be a somewhat dangerous proposition, if the message is not on point and to the right audience at the right time.

However when done correctly, there's the potential to hit a home run with the power of direct one-to-one personalized contact.

Another digital advertising channel that is typically not as widely known or used, especially by small and medium-sized businesses, is *affiliate marketing*. This digital marketing channel allows an organization to tap into a network of digital publishers to help sell their product.

There are a number of affiliate marketing networks that bring thousands of network advertisers and websites who are looking for products to sell. Just as with email and mobile marketing, it's essential to identify the proper audience within the associated networks in order to offer the right product to that audience.

Leveraging these massive networks of passionate fans has the potential to help grow the audience for a product or service in a rapid fashion. Affiliate marketing is definitely one channel that I would recommend any small or medium-sized business investigate, but certainly conduct your due diligence before proceeding.

Within digital advertising, there are five primary methods of delivery available for advertisers.

Sponsored Search

Advertisers bid on keywords and create text-based or display ad campaigns for their product or service featuring those keywords.

Search engines typically show a number of sponsored search ads either above, in between, on the side or below search engine results. Since search is typically where the majority of all consumer traffic comes from, the available impressions for most keywords can be quite large and offer an opportunity to attract a proportionally sizable audience.

Display Advertising

Display ads are image or video-based content used to promote a product or service. Digital display advertising features many shapes and sizes of creative that can be displayed in numerous locations on a web page.

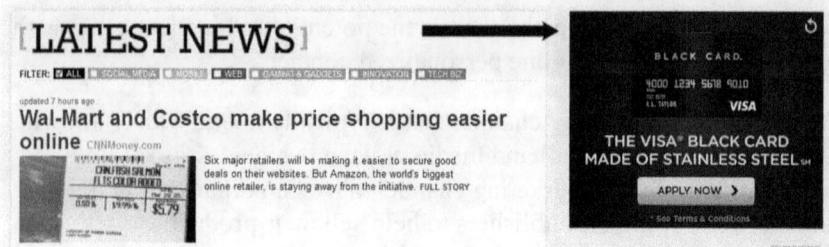

As a larger push to mobile devices has been made over the past few years, advertisers are seeing challenges and opportunities to promote their products using display ads. Although optimal size for display ads on mobile devices is much smaller on average as compared to traditional computer screens, channel operators have continued to think creatively to help their advertisers successfully reach this audience with the best experience possible.

Pop-Ups and Pop-Unders

An ancillary method of delivery for digital advertising is pop-ups or pop unders that launch a new browser window in sequence with the loading of a new web page. Pop-ups and pop unders have been around for over a decade and have seen their popularity rise, fall, and rise again in that time.

In recent years, as consumers have become more savvy with their information consumption, these types of new browser window applications have actually become more popular for publishers. Although they don't provide everyone with a preferred experience, recent tests and studies have shown that they have proven effective for lead generation campaigns with the right audience and the right message.

Interstitial Advertising

This is a form of a pop-up that appears before a selected piece of content, and is often a prerequisite before advancing to the requested content piece. This extra level of forced engagement can sometimes rub consumers the wrong way. However, if it's used in front of the right content, which is often a form of premium content, most readers have become accustomed to patiently sitting through the promotion to see their requested information.

Video Pre-Roll Advertising

As bandwidth has increased for the average consumer, on both computer and mobile devices, new opportunities continue to evolve for digital advertising. One of these is video pre-roll advertising, which are short clips that appear before requested video content. A positive element of pre-roll is that the requested video content will appear in the same video player as the pre-roll content, so consumers are not forced to click away from or into another device.

YouTube has used five-second minimum watch times for some advertising pre-roll before their hosted videos. As an advertiser, it's good to realize that five-second minimum watches require an immediate impact to retain viewers for an extended view of their promotion.

Some platforms have tested requiring viewers to choose an advertisement out of a selection of ads to watch before they get to their requested content. As with most of these methods of delivery, there is typically immediate pushback from consumers, but that negative response often dies down as the consumers become more accustomed to this method of promotion.

Benefits of Digital Advertising

I like to compare digital advertising to outdoor or billboard ads. They allow an advertiser the opportunity to reach a new audience with targeted promotion with the potential to quickly increase brand awareness.

The ability to provide immediate impact can be a valuable tool, especially for new and growing small and medium-sized businesses who are looking to rapidly grow their customer base. If you can select the appropriate channel and deliver a properly aligned message, you can start sending qualified traffic to your website immediately upon the launch of your digital advertising campaigns.

Since you're helping educate consumers about yourself and your product or service before they even take a step towards learning more about you, the traffic from paid search is often well qualified, with the potential for solid engagement with your product or service. Being able to filter out a good match amongst consumers for your business is essential because it helps you maximize your time towards assisting quality potential customers.

Another benefit of digital advertising is its ability to define a solid forecasted cost of implementation. Whether you're looking for sponsored search advertising, social media marketing, or even display advertising, you can set a budget and receive a forecasted number of clicks or traffic to your website based upon your potential investment. You can even set your budget on a daily, weekly, or monthly basis so that you can stick to your plan and adjust accordingly based upon the research and results.

As you create and execute this plan, what makes digital advertising such an awesome opportunity is the fact that it is extremely measurable, lending itself towards optimizing your investment. When you know how consumers are reacting to a message or an offer in near real time, you're much better equipped to refine your approach. Actively assessing what's working and what's not working as it happens is standard with digital advertising, unlike many traditional media channels where there can be a significant lag time between campaign creation, execution, and collection of the results. With digital advertising you can create a campaign, launch it, and see the results—all before lunch.

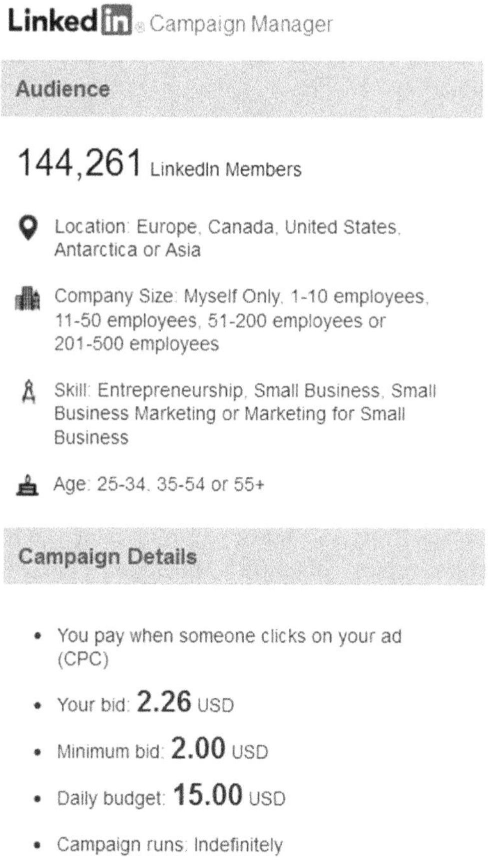

Linked in ® Campaign Manager

Audience

144,261 LinkedIn Members

- Location: Europe, Canada, United States, Antarctica or Asia

- Company Size: Myself Only, 1-10 employees, 11-50 employees, 51-200 employees or 201-500 employees

- Skill: Entrepreneurship, Small Business, Small Business Marketing or Marketing for Small Business

- Age: 25-34, 35-54 or 55+

Campaign Details

- You pay when someone clicks on your ad (CPC)
- Your bid: **2.26** USD
- Minimum bid: **2.00** USD
- Daily budget: **15.00** USD
- Campaign runs: Indefinitely

In addition to measurability, most digital channels offer highly targeted options to segment audiences and help you pinpoint your exact sweet spot. Advertisers can choose geographic and demographic segmentation, along with specific events to help completely define the who, where, and when they want their message to be seen. Having this powerful ability to target and then measure is a great opportunity for small and medium-sized businesses, because it allows you to maximize the potential of your budget. The costs of testing digital ads can be minimized and the speed with which you can execute is unprecedented.

Another benefit of digital advertising is the variety of options that are available and the tools that marketers now have to produce successful campaigns. There are various ad formats, timing options, and channel options for nearly every product or service.

A secondary benefit of digital advertising can be researching new products and services or additional business challenges by crowdsourcing an audience. For example, businesses often use sponsored search or display ads to test product names or even product ideas to gauge a response before the product is created. When you have a massive audience of people at your disposal there is a great opportunity to gauge their interest to help with decision-making for your organization.

Remarketing Campaigns

Advertising networks are also offering advertisers the ability to create what are known as *remarketing campaigns* that help identify and reinforce your messaging to the right consumer. Remarketing lets you show ads to users who've previously visited your website as they browse the Web.

When you use remarketing, you'll tag pages of your site that correspond to certain products or services you want to promote. For example, you could add a "dishwasher" tag on all of the pages where you sell dishwashers.

The second step of remarketing is to create a digital ad campaign to show ads for your dishwasher to people who've previously visited these pages as they browse sites across ad networks.

This is a powerful tool and one that many businesses have used to achieve solid results. As with nearly all digital marketing, the more customized and segmented the message and the audience, the better the return on investment. This message reinforcement will continue to remind the consumer about your product long after they have left your site.

Paying for Digital Advertising

Purchasing digital advertising, just as the platforms and the methods of deliveries, comes in a number of different options. Most sponsored search is based around a real-time auction format. Advertisers can bid for a particular keyword and can receive suggested minimum bid estimates from the search engines.

Advertisers can choose to pay per impression (PPI), pay per click to their website (PPC), pay per view (PPV), or pay per action (PPA). A cost-per-action format is typically used for lead generation purposes, when an organization is looking to find potential buyers for their product or service. If a consumer completes an online form, the advertiser will then pay the website or publisher for the completed form.

Challenges of Digital Advertising

We've talked at length about the benefits of digital advertising, so what are the challenges? A primary challenge for digital advertising is the fact that success is based upon testing and optimization. What this means is a lot of work goes into creating an efficient and effective digital advertising campaign. Although you may be involved in a real-time auction for sponsored search or display advertising, there are multiple factors that go into how much you pay and how many impressions or how much exposure you'll receive.

The reality is, digital advertising requires solid experience and a systematized approach to test and optimize each element of the advertising campaign. This includes the subject line of the sponsored search ad, the text or copy of the ad, and any other component within the advertisement.

Adding to the complexity, the rules for success on each advertising platform are slightly different. What works on Google AdWords is slightly different than what works when advertising on LinkedIn. So it's important to test and optimize for each advertising platform and not to assume that each ad or copy will work in each scenario.

For most auction-based advertising channels, advertisers are rewarded for their *click-through rate*, which is produced by the relevancy of the ad and the landing page that consumers are directed to after they click on the ad. Advertising platforms will judge the quality of the landing page by how relevant it is to the ad that you're referring to. The better the relevancy, the higher the potential to be ranked higher within the paid advertisements.

This places a great deal of pressure on the advertiser to consistently hit the mark with their ads and their landing pages. Another challenge is the fact that banners can sometimes see a decrease in performance as consumers grow accustomed to them. This isn't always the case, but it can be accentuated on certain platforms. Revised creative is often needed to continue generating a consistent amount of traffic to your website.

If you're bidding on certain popular keywords, you may have to pay handsomely for those keywords to drive traffic to your site. This supply-versus-demand model is an advantage for the ad platform, as they have a number of suitors for these highly important keywords.

If you can't afford the going rate for these keywords, you may want to think in terms of *long-tail keywords*, which are groups of words or even a sentence that still targets your audience, but will more than likely attract fewer searches. The advantage here is the price for the long-tail keywords can often be dramatically lower than the price for single or head keywords.

**FOR THIS BONUS
ONLINE CONTENT VISIT**
walterlis.com/resources

A promising area of advancement and growth within paid search or digital advertising, are **tools to manage your digital advertising accounts**. Keeping a number of plates spinning across digital advertising as well as all your marketing platforms is a constant challenge for marketers. But just as in many other areas of marketing, the necessity for tools to help manage or automate processes has produced some tremendous new solutions that are helping businesses. As more options become available for digital advertising, it becomes inherent upon the marketer to become more precise and better organized to manage their efforts and produce consistent and effective results.

Chapter 7

Social Media Marketing

I like to use the analogy of a food truck to describe the opportunity available through social media marketing. If you own a food truck, it's your job to sync your menu with the audience that you'll be visiting. Consequently, if your culinary specialties involve a lot of meat products, you're not going to want to drive your truck into a neighborhood populated by vegetarians.

The same philosophy applies with social media channels. The audience is different for each channel, meaning you'll decide to park your truck there depending upon whether they're a good potential audience for your product or service.

Participation in social media has been growing exponentially over the past decade. The potential channels within social media have followed suit as well. This makes it essential for the SMB owner to identify where they might be able to reach the relevant audience.

The first question you have to ask is what are the objectives of each social media site? Are my potential customers a good fit with this channel? Do the people who need my product or service spend significant time on this social media channel? Bring your product to the wrong channel and it could be like bringing sand to the beach.

In addition to identifying which channel and whether their audience is appropriate for your product or service, you also need to know the ground rules that are involved with each social media channel. For example, in some networks it's more appropriate or accepted to talk about business opportunities then on other networks. A network such as LinkedIn is focused on business and careers, making it traditionally a good fit for business-to-business lead generation. However, if you don't follow each site's own ground rules, you'll have a short lifespan and limited success.

The reality with social media marketing is that you have no control over the audience, the rules, or the social media network itself. Everyone is a guest, from the participants to the sponsors. In fact, the audience information is owned by the social media channel itself. Any channel can restrict your access if you don't obey their rules, causing you to potentially lose the audience that you've created on their network.

As I mentioned earlier in the book, this rent-to own model means that until you can capture them, you are renting your audience on any social media channel. You might ask, "Then why am I getting involved with social media in the first place?" The answer is that it's a lot easier going to where the audience is than building your own network. You have to go where your potential customers are spending their time with the primary goal of transitioning your audience on that platform to your website, where you'll own the relationship.

The primary benefit of social media marketing is that you can efficiently build your audience by reaching new potential customers. You may not own this new contact directly at first, but you can certainly create awareness and take steps to accentuate the know, like, and trust factors, with the goal of transferring your new relationships into a different environment where you'll have more control.

With social media marketing you can also gather marketplace intelligence to help identify potential opportunities for your product or service. If there's a large group of people talking about a specific pain point or issue that revolves around your business or industry, you can become involved in the conversation or you can even just utilize the questions that people are asking to improve your customer service plan. If you choose to get involved in the discussion, this is a great opportunity to create and/or continue engagement with an audience.

By inserting yourself into a discussion, you can build your thought leadership within the marketplace. Assisting customers or potential customers through social media is a great way to help the community by sharing your expertise. It's also a great way to build trust, even with people who aren't actively participating in the conversation but are reading your feedback and guidance.

Another benefit of social media marketing is that it can assist with search engine optimization. As discussed previously, one of the aspects of search engine algorithms is social proof. When you create content within a social media channel that is subsequently shared, you can help boost your authority in the eyes of the search engines. Having "sharing icons" for all the major social media channels on your website helps you encourage your readers to share your thought leadership across their social media landscape, therefore assisting in your efforts to boost social media and SEO authority.

The Mental Trick That Will Help You Fall Asleep, Fast

By Shelby Freedman Harris, Psy.D. for YouBeauty.com

We've all been there. You're lying in bed, exhausted, stressed and staring at the clock, counting down how much time you have left before your alarm goes off. Chances are, stress is what woke you up early in the first place and now the stress of getting too little sleep is keeping you awake.

It's no surprise that one of the most common triggers for insomnia is stress -- both good and bad. Stress comes from thinking about the past or worrying about the future, losing track of being in the moment. I commonly hear patients tell me that when they get in bed at night to try and sleep, their brains don't stop and instead they're thinking of the day, what didn't get done, what needs to get done and any other pressing or mundane issues in life.

However, probably the biggest overall benefit of social media marketing is helping with lead generation and sales. Improving your reach and overall awareness within your industry is a positive byproduct of participating in the appropriate social media worlds. If you participate correctly and assist others by using your resources and knowledge, you can create a direct conduit from a social media channel into a lead and convert that person eventually into a sale and happy customer. This is typically not a quick or easy process, but it is a great way to use an already available network to expand your customer base.

Challenges of Social Media

One of the biggest challenges of social media marketing is that engaging in a conversation and participating in a social network, let alone multiple social networks, can take time. The process of identifying opportunities within social media, and then creating content that fits the rules and appeals to the proper audience, can be daunting.

In addition, it's essential to measure the effect of social media marketing, which also can be a bit tricky. Since you're engaging with audiences on a closed platform, you're often limited to their analytics and reports provided by that social media network. Therefore, you have to be prepared to use *outside tools and services* to develop a method to measure the impact of each channel on your bottom line.

**FOR THIS BONUS
ONLINE CONTENT VISIT**
walterlis.com/resources

Where and how you should be focusing your efforts within social media is ultimately the biggest question. For example, you may think that all signs point to becoming involved on Facebook, but once you start to pour your resources into that channel, you could find a different result. As with all digital marketing, be sure to test and measure your work within social media so you can quickly adjust based on the results.

Another challenge with social media marketing is converting your thought leadership into leads and sales. Each step of the process—from identifying an audience, to engaging that audience, to utilizing the know-like-trust factor—has to be followed in order. You typically can't jump over or eliminate a stage, so it's important to have a thoughtful process in channel recognition so you can continue to move contacts from leads into sales.

One additional challenge with social media marketing comes from the fact that the social networks can often offer a level of anonymity that can sometimes produce negative or even damaging comments about a business, whether they're true or false. Overcoming these negative voices and not allowing them to dilute your brand reputation has become an essential component of any solid social media strategy.

Success Strategies

There are many keys to success within social media marketing. It's essential to set up a closed-loop tracking environment to identify impact by social media channel. You have to be able to track your efforts that go on in each channel, all the way through to lead generation on your website and into sales. If you don't have a clean path from start to finish, it's difficult to assess the impact that you're making in that social media channel.

It's also essential to optimize everything that you're doing within social media marketing, just as it is in all digital marketing. You'll need to be testing your strategies and tracking their results with the goal of improving performance and getting more bang for your buck.

To be successful with your social media strategy, start with a disciplined process schedule to avoid over-investment until you've identified success. What this means is you can't allow yourself to be pulled into spending time or money on something that may or may not work properly. Therefore, developing strict processes and schedules to manage resources for each social media channel can be the difference between overall success and failure.

FOR THIS BONUS ONLINE CONTENT VISIT
walterlis.com/resources

When possible, it's a great idea to use *tools to manage your social media presence*. This is especially true for small and medium-sized businesses that are looking to create as much impact as a Fortune 500 company but with significantly less resources. The tools available in this area are getting better by the day in helping level the playing field so that small and medium-sized businesses can compete by using their resources in a smart and intelligent fashion.

It's always important to consistently create content in the style and format that matches each platform. This is a golden rule, because the style changes for each social media network. Some social media channels may do better with more visual content while others prefer text-based information. Others may work better with short succinct messaging while they struggle with more vivid content such as video.

It's essential to integrate your search engine optimization efforts into your social media plan. As mentioned previously, social media can be a great assistance to your SEO by providing the opportunity for social media proof. When creating content, and when deciding upon what to create, it's a good idea to cross-check to see what you can do to assist in the social media efforts. If there is a specific topic that you're looking to improve your rankings in, you can create more content for relevant social media channels to help assist in developing social media shares and even back links to your website.

It's impossible to ignore the importance of using your social media channels to drive activation to your website. Your participation in social media is a great way of building an audience; however, you're only renting that audience. The path to owning the relationship with that audience is to transform the conversation to your website. Only then can you begin a one-to-one customized relationship with that lead or potential customer.

Never forget that you have to play by the rules for each social media channel. Many organizations have put a great deal of effort and resources into creating an audience on a social media channel, only to have their audience taken away and their presence eliminated because they did not follow the rules and guidelines set by the social media network. You are a visitor to that social media channel, so be sure to learn and follow their rules.

Consider developing best practices for your organization for each social media channel. You may share responsibilities for posting content on a social media network within your organization. In order to keep a similar voice and message, you'll want to have a set of rules and guidelines for your team to follow so that the message stays consistent.

And finally it's a good idea to have a clear policy on how to address negative comments or feedback that you might receive through social media. This should be part of your guideline strategy for anyone tasked with the responsibility of posting to your social media networks. It's best to be prepared for circumstances that could harm the integrity or reputation of your organization.

Chapter 8

Analytics

One of the strengths of digital marketing is the ability to use analytics and data to help manage your marketing and business decisions pragmatically. For SMBs, this can be a tremendous tool to build efficiency. The key to developing a successful digital analytics program for your business is creating a closed-loop system that allows you to track the impact each digital channel makes on your objective.

A primary benefit of using digital analytics is that it allows you to avoid making assumptions. Having the ability to identify clearly what is happening within your marketing campaigns and then turn that into usable insights can help create efficiencies within your organization. This type of data allows you to quickly identify inefficiencies and improve the overall capabilities of your organization.

Once you can see the performance statistics and how consumers are reacting to your marketing campaigns, the next step is to define and attribute what is driving that impact. For example, if you're looking to improve your lead generation, you need to know what sources are performing the best in terms of driving new potential leads to your organization.

Is your email marketing campaign sending more people to your website then your social media efforts? Are you receiving most of your leads via the search engines? Or are your paid digital advertising campaigns bringing the most new customers and new leads to your organization?

With the ***tools now available for digital analytics***, you're able to see results across all channels, platforms, hardware, and software. What this means is that you can compare and contrast where your efforts and your investment should be going, with the goal of optimizing both elements.

**FOR THIS BONUS
ONLINE CONTENT VISIT**
walterlis.com/resources

Tracking your results across all sources is a key differentiator between an optimized business and one that is in a set-it-and-forget-it mode. The difference between these two organizations is that one is constantly improving results and lowering costs while the other is continuing to hope for better results while seeing their costs increase.

Analytical Resources

One of the best resources for useful analytical information is the internal site search results on your website. This is a great place to see what visitors on your site are looking for. What they type into the search box on your site could lead you to new products, ideas, and better ways to present your information.

For example, if you're seeing a number of searches for a competitor's products on your website, you may decide to change the way you're presenting your information, or create additional information that can help answer the differences between your product and your competitors. Assisting the visitors on your website with finding what they need should always be job one.

Your digital analytics tracking also has to be able to assess the opportunities across various sources. Examples of these include:

• Social media campaigns

• Email marketing

• Paid advertising (mobile-based advertising, video)

Another primary benefit of creating a closed loop digital analytics system is the opportunity assessment that you'll be able to provide using your data. Top digital analytics tools, like Google Analytics, provide all the keys and clues necessary to identify where opportunities may exist. Whether your customers want more information, a wider array of products, or might not be interested in a potential product that you're considering can be seen by properly utilizing your digital analytics.

By implementing the insights taken from this information, you can also use this new knowledge to help assist in setting your business goals. If you see that a specific topic on your site is attracting a lot of interest, then you may decide to invest further in your organization's involvement with that product. Likewise, if you see that there is a great demand on other websites for a new product that you don't currently offer, you may decide that you would like to focus your organization's efforts towards that area.

Taking all this information into account and implementing a closed loop system to track all the various components of your digital marketing will allow you to make educated decisions that can seriously improve the performance of your organization. However, it's important to understand that the data you get back is only as good as the data you put in. Meaning, setting up your analytics at the outset in the proper format so nothing gets lost will be key to your success.

Analytics vs. Assumptions

I mentioned earlier in the book that business decisions must be driven by facts, not conjecture. For an existing business that wants to take their digital marketing to the next level, one of the hardest things is to get away from internal decisions built on assumptions. Business owners might feel as though their expertise is what should be driving all decisions, including those made online. While this expertise will be vital to creating a coherent and consistent message for digital consumers, using assumptions or an assumptive-based process can defeat the purpose of what digital analytics can provide.

If you know how consumers are reacting to an offer or a new product, then you'll have actionable insights and real-world data on their preferences. At times, this may go against what you expected or what your experience tells you. Having the courage to trust what the consumers are telling you can be a challenge for many small and medium-sized businesses.

In addition to getting away from making assumptions, another challenge that small and medium-sized business owners often face with regard to analytics-based decision making is being overloaded by too much information. As mentioned previously, tools such as Google Analytics are capable of tracking an exorbitant amount of data on the behavior of your audience. Becoming overwhelmed and subsequently suffering from paralysis by analysis is obviously not a helpful reaction.

Paring down the information, and more precisely identifying the key drivers that are triggering success or failure, is paramount in a successful approach towards your digital analytics. Often times, finding the key performance indicators and creating simplified dashboards so that everyone within the organization knows what's happening can lead to major gains in performance and communication.

Source Attribution

Another challenge within digital marketing campaign management can be attributing the source of a final sale. Since a customer may receive multiple emails, social media connections, digital advertising messages, and even off-line or real-world communication with your organization, it can be quite challenging to decide who or what channel should receive attribution for finally converting that lead into a sale.

Although source attribution is considered the Holy Grail for identifying the most impactful components of your marketing, I often recommend allowing this to develop organically instead of focusing a great deal of time and attention toward solving this problem. As you might anticipate, attribution can be one of the more complicated challenges that any organization will face. However, as your digital marketing campaigns progress, you'll have more data and more experience to better identify the key drivers in this formula.

Knowing where *not* to focus your efforts is often just as important as knowing where to focus them. Organizations can sometimes choose to place emphasis on the wrong key performance indicators or the wrong metrics when assessing the performance of their digital marketing.

Identifying social media marketing success by the number of likes on Facebook or the number of followers on Twitter is a simple example of a misplaced priority. While growing these two metrics can be helpful, they should not be considered key determinants towards the success of your campaigns because the impact they make is often much further towards the top of the funnel. Crafting engaging communications via email during a one-on-one dialogue with a customer at the bottom of your digital marketing funnel is an example of a focus item that will often have a much bigger impact on generating leads and sales.

When identifying key performance indicators (KPIs) within digital analytics, you'll be looking for information that is *relevant, timely* and *useful*. Asking yourself these three questions as you assemble your digital marketing dashboard will help determine the key growth triggers and issues that need to be monitored.

Another challenge organizations may face is lacking benchmarks for comparing their digital marketing efforts. Google Analytics offers some benchmarking capabilities that you can use as you craft your campaigns. However, your organization or your products or services may be a little bit different than what's available, which could create a challenge in identifying not only what you should be tracking but how your efforts are working compared to your competitors.

Your analytics dashboard has to be created so that everyone within the organization can use and understand it. Whether you're in finance, management, marketing, or sales, it's essential to have valuable data that is easy to understand and can assist each business unit and provide them with real-time information and insights.

It's often better to create multiple marketing dashboards that provide key performance indicators for each of the various business units within your organization. For example, your sales department will probably be more interested in the engagement that consumers are having toward specific products. Having this information will allow them to focus their efforts more keenly on the products or services that are drawing the most attention, and therefore provide the opportunity for low hanging fruit.

Five Key Metrics

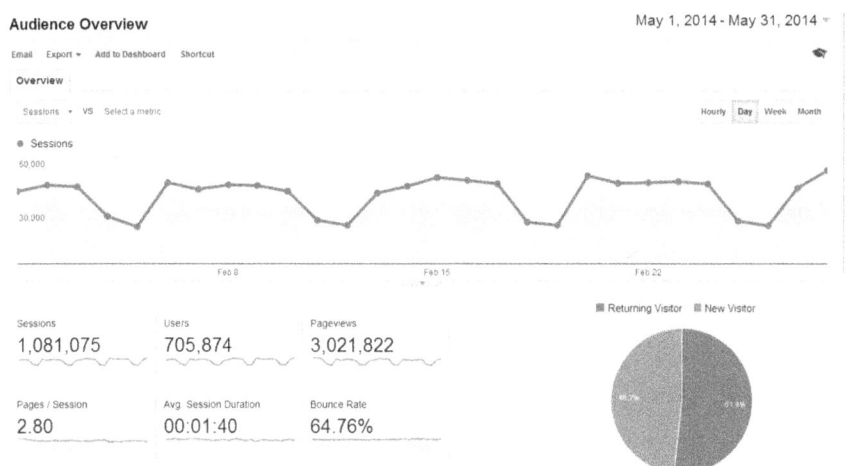

Here are five simple yet important metrics that can benefit most organizations and give you valuable insights. In early 2014, Google Analytics changed the terminology they use within the reports to change what they call "visits" and "unique visitors." Now, visits is named "sessions" and unique visitors is named "users."

1. Users (formerly unique visitors). This is a single person visiting your site. When you use the metric unique visitor, that typically means how many times or how many people have visited your site.

2. Sessions (formerly visits). As opposed to unique visitors, visits can include multiple visits made by a single person to your website. A single individual can visit a website ten times in one day, while a unique visitor can only visit your website once.

3. Time on your website. Identifying how long people are spending on your website is a great indicator for the relevance, or stickiness of your website. If your audience is spending a minute or less on your site, there's a good chance that the information that you're providing is not proving to be engaging or valuable enough for them. Keeping an eye on this metric as you make changes or add new content to your site will give you an idea as to the overall success of your content marketing efforts.

4. Bounce rate. When visitors come to your website, visit just one page, and then leave, this is known as a bounce. A high bounce rate is a key indicator that a visitor has received very limited value from your website. It's a great indicator that something is missing on your site. It could be that you're not providing enough information or you might be attracting a poorly matched audience to your site. Lowering your bounce rate should always be a target goal as you build your content marketing efforts.

5. Conversion rate. This is converting visitors to your website to achieve your final end goal, whether that is gathering lead information or making a sale. Your conversion rate is a prime indicator of success for your overall digital marketing effort. Monitoring the conversion rate of each segment of your marketing will lead to better site optimization.

For example, if you're looking to convert a visitor on your website into a lead by collecting their contact information, there are multiple attributes that you'll want to monitor. For example, when people get to a specific landing page on your site, how long are they spending on that page? Are they clicking on the call to action? If you have a form on your website that has three fields versus four fields, is the extra field positively or negatively affecting the number of people who register? Using conversion rate optimization throughout your digital marketing will help you reduce friction and drastically improve your overall success.

Opportunity Analysis

Using your digital analytics to provide clues of potential opportunities is a major benefit that most off-line marketing strategies aren't able to provide. By monitoring your digital key performance indicators as well as your site search, you can quickly compare potential scenarios by identifying the preferences of your audience.

Are the various components of your site optimized properly? Are you getting enough leads from the white paper that you've created, or are your landing pages not converting as well as you might expect?

In addition to your own internal analysis, you can use your digital analytics to provide competitive analysis. Identifying what your customers prefer is of great benefit to your plans in your strategy.

Opportunity analysis can be triggered by successful testing within all of your digital marketing. Since we're just moving pixels around, the opportunity cost or the investment cost is traditionally low within digital marketing. There are numerous *testing and optimization tools* that can help improve your testing capabilities.

**FOR THIS BONUS
ONLINE CONTENT VISIT**
walterlis.com/resources

A common motto digital marketers use is "fail fast." What they mean by this is since tests and changes are easy to make, it's in your best interest to quickly find out what works, or find out what doesn't work, and get rid of it.

There are two main types of testing within digital marketing. The first is called an *A/B split test*. This is when a single variable is compared with two tests conducted in parallel.

For example, I may create two versions of a single landing page with two different headlines. Based upon my analytics, I will keep the headline that converts the best, and remove the lower converting headline, replacing it with another test version. I'll continue this process to incrementally enhance the overall efficiency of that page.

The other major type of testing is what's called *multivariate testing*. This is when you compare multiple variables and how they interact with each other. Multivariate testing is often beneficial when you're testing more advanced designs or strategies.

Since there is such a wide breadth and depth of digital marketing channels, it's only appropriate that we have a wide depth and breadth of *tools for collecting and assessing your digital analytics*. At the forefront of these tools are those that monitor website traffic, such as Google Analytics or Adobe Site Catalyst.

**FOR THIS BONUS
ONLINE CONTENT VISIT**
walterlis.com/resources

The introduction of Google Analytics in 2005 provided a powerful tool with no cost to the user, and was a watershed moment for the field of digital marketing. It brought a world-class suite of tools and capabilities that are excellent for both inexperienced and highly experienced digital marketers. Until that time, assessing the performance of your website often involved reading endless log file reports.

With Google Analytics, any small or medium-sized business has access to a free, easy-to-use resource that can be quickly and easily implemented on their website. The data and information that it provides can truly help shape the success of your business online.

In addition to website traffic, there are tools available that can track the analytics of your search engine optimization efforts. These products often include link analysis tools that identify the back links pointing to your company's website.

Likewise, social media analysis tools have become quite popular as organizations look to quantify their efforts and identify the marketplace availability within a social media channel. There are numerous tools available that can help you manage your accounts and assist in identifying what's working and what's not within social media.

As we've discussed, both your email marketing efforts and your digital advertising efforts need to be scrutinized diligently. When you're investing time and resources towards creating campaigns for either of these two channels, your success or failure often hinges on the quality of performance data that you're able to assemble.

Chapter 9

Demand Generation

Demand generation means creating awareness of a problem, need or challenge in the marketplace. You're looking to enlighten an audience to a current or potential issue for which you have a solution. Creating this type of spark isn't easy, but it's essential if you have a new product or service that people aren't familiar with and don't understand the benefits of. Successful demand generation programs often work best when they're able to convey a simple message to let people know what they could be missing.

Demand generation isn't usually necessary for a well-known, existing product that most people are familiar with. But in those situations where you are looking to build something new and need to educate the public about the problem and solution, demand generation is a must.

Demand generation can be relevant to an individual solution or product. It can also be relevant for an entire industry. For example, if a new type of power generation becomes available for consumers in their homes, then the power generation provider needs to enlighten their target audience so they become aware of the benefits of this new option. This type of demand generation includes a large component of education, as you are bringing a new concept or approach to people's lives.

The goals of demand generation begin with identifying the awareness of your audience to your product. Do they know they have a problem? If they're not aware of the problem, they probably won't be interested in your product or solution.

Finding whom your solution can help the most can often be the most important predictor of success.

Identifying the audience that can benefit most by what your product or solution can provide is the first step.

Targeting your demand generation efforts or your education towards these folks is the second step.

Is your audience aware of the problem? Did you know that you may be missing this important part of your house? This type of question/answer strategy leads a consumer to ask themselves about their understanding of the situation.

Problem and Solution

When creating your demand generation programs, you're looking to help others consider if they have the *problem* that your product or service can help resolve.

The second stage of the process is to present the *solution* that you can provide. These two parts—the question and the answer—are tied together and have to be easily connected in your campaigns.

If you can connect one with the other, then you can begin to connect your brand to the problem. Companies that have had success with connecting their brands to a specific problem have historically been able to capture a large share of the market as people immediately associate their specific brand with this issue even though there may be multiple other products that can solve the same problem. This is a first-mover advantage that can pay huge dividends down the road.

Another major goal of demand generation is to create interest by changing perspectives. Your audience may not beware of improvements or changes within the industry that you service. A solid demand generation campaign would consist of promotion and support for not only your company and your products, but for your industry as well. Changing the perspectives of customers about your industry as well as your products or service can lead to both industry and organizational growth.

The final goal of your demand generation campaign should be to funnel activated consumers into your lead generation component. If your demand generation campaigns do their job successfully, the end result will be interest in the products or solutions that you can provide to solve the problems that you've highlighted. Your demand generation efforts, while noteworthy, won't be largely beneficial to your organization unless you can convert them into leads.

Create Awareness

The challenges of demand generation programs typically revolve around simplifying the problem or need that you're looking to explain to your audience. Depending upon the complexity of the problem, it could be hard to explain to consumers what the real benefits of your product are. This can be a challenge for those individuals who are very familiar with your industry, let alone people who are not that familiar with what you're providing.

Disrupt the Status Quo

In addition to overcoming the challenge of complexity, demand generation campaigns are looking to cause a disruption in the status quo. Consumers are creatures of habit and are used to their specific routines of content consumption. When you're generating demand, you are inherently looking to disrupt those patterns and insert your message into the content stream. Creating this disruption and producing valuable messaging effectively can be one of the biggest challenges of all of your marketing campaigns.

As we mentioned previously, a large part of demand generation is creating engaging content that presents your solution to the problem that you've identified and then helps establish awareness of your brand. Identifying what type of content to create and develop in a way that is easily digestible for the audience can be a major challenge. You'll need to know how your audience prefers to consume their content, and you'll have to continue to test to see what works and what resonates with your target groups.

Build the Relationship

And finally, after you're able to create awareness and disrupt the status quo, your last job is to direct that audience into your lead generation email workflow tracks. You've stirred up the pot enough to make consumers aware of what you can do. The final, and most important part, is to have a cohesive plan in order to guide people to take the next step and begin a relationship with your organization.

Lead Generation

Digital lead generation is collecting contact information using online request forms from individuals who are potential customers for your product or service. Organizations have been managing lead generation programs for decades. But with the advent of digital marketing and the latest digital marketing tools, we've seen a seismic shift in what can be achieved in this area.

The goal of lead generation through digital marketing is to find relevant potential customers who could benefit from your product or service. Attracting the wrong audience isn't helpful, and therefore from the outset the focus should be on relevant potential customers. Having poorly correlated leads to follow up with can cost your team time and money chasing after people who don't need or want what you have to offer.

Another goal of lead generation is to collect the right mix of personal data from your online forms. If people download a report or white paper that you've created, there is often a fine line between asking for too little information and asking for too much information. Ask for too little, and you'll have less information to customize your follow-up message. Ask for too much information and you could turn people off who are unwilling to make that trade of their contact information for your information product.

Therefore it's essential to identify what data points are necessary to distinguish solid potential targets. You're looking to eliminate poor matches for your product or service, or people who are not interested in what you have to offer, as well as your competitors. You're also looking to determine what stage of the customer journey each lead is at.

From my experience, I've seen that there is a direct correlation between the quality of information product or lead magnet with how much information people are willing to provide. The higher quality you can offer, the more leads you can attract.

Testing to Optimize

It's a good guideline when starting out to test multiple versions of your forms with each lead magnet. For example, I'll have a form that has four fields such as name, email address, phone number and company, and then I'll test another form with five fields adding an additional field such as company website, for the same product. Once you have a statistically viable amount of traffic sent to both pages, you'll be able to identify if there is a breaking point at which people will stop registering to download your offer.

As we've talked about at length in this book, this continuous optimization is at the core of all digital marketing. We don't have to make assumptions, and we certainly don't have to guess what works best. It's no different when deciding how many fields you should have in a form in order to optimize your lead generation efforts.

What benefits does lead generation provide for an organization? Having a permission-based digital lead generation system often results in having higher conversion success rates than typical sales outreach efforts such as cold calling because the lead generation prospects are prequalified. Your digital lead generation efforts typically come from an exchange of your expertise for your lead's contact information.

If people are not interested in the subject that you're writing about, they will typically not seek to learn more about that subject. This means your lead generation efforts inherently are an effective way to prequalify your leads and determine who you should be focusing your efforts on.

An additional benefit of lead generation is the ability to target specific geographic and demographic audiences for your product or service. All of the digital marketing strategies that we've discussed previously such as paid search marketing, social media marketing, and search engine optimization have a great deal of very finite targeting capabilities. You know whom you are getting your message in front of, often times down to the smallest level of detail.

Having this level of detail allows you to pinpoint your efforts when looking to generate leads. You can easily correlate a product or service to the digital marketing channel that works best. We find out which channel works best by testing.

Determining the Cost

You're also able to determine the cost of your efforts on a per-lead basis because of your closed loop digital analytics. This can be a very effective tool for small and medium-sized business as you look to determine cost-effective approaches to grow your business. Off-line lead generation typically doesn't allow for a closed loop system in which you can trace the exact amount of money invested and the return on that investment in real time.

The takeaway here is that a company can take control of the top of their business development funnel by creating impactful lead generation campaigns. You can choose the product or service that you wish to offer to prospects and leverage the corresponding performance data to determine what aligns best with your business goals.

The challenge of lead generation through digital marketing can be in identifying quality leads. For example, by offering quality educational downloads for your business, you could attract researchers, competitors, and non-buyers just as easily as you could attract decision-makers who could buy your product or service.

What's important to understand, however, is your lead generation efforts are not the only source of data. They are the beginning of your entire lead development campaign. The primary goal is to get the best qualified contacts you can find into your lead funnel, and then you will be able to further refine your knowledge and information about these folks as you head into lead nurturing campaigns.

Collecting proper data will be at the forefront of your lead generation campaigns. It goes without saying that you'll need to have this information in an easy-to-access format so that this data does not get compromised throughout your organization as it is shared amongst departments.

A Fast Response Is Key

It's also imperative that you create an internal system for immediate response once you generate a lead. The odds of reaching a lead are a hundred times greater when they are contacted within five minutes after they submit your form than if they are contacted thirty minutes after they submit your form. This is a huge disparity and an obvious reward for having your system calibrated to the highest efficiency possible.

The odds that a lead will move through your sales process are twenty times greater if you make contact with that lead within five minutes as compared to thirty minutes. In the digital realm, most consumers and buyers are in an active stage even during initial stages of research. Even if you collect the minimal amount of information in your online forms, you'll be rewarded handsomely if you can follow up immediately on those leads.

Don't allow you or your organization to get overwhelmed by all of the potential data that is involved in your lead generation products. It's a necessity to continue to create new content and lead magnets, but I highly recommend that you wait to test your initial lead magnets in order to learn as to what that may or may not attract.

Lead Nurturing

Lead nurturing is the process of growing and building relationships with potential clients no matter what stage they are at in their customer journey. Digital marketing lead nurturing campaigns have made major strides in improving the efficiency of demand generation, lead generation, and developing sales for organizations.

Today's technology has drastically changed what can be accomplished through digital marketing nurturing campaigns. The disparity between the companies that use lead nurturing versus those that don't is getting larger, as the organizations that learn how to leverage this tool are rapidly grabbing market share while their competitors are left in their wake.

In a perfect world, every business would have a single dedicated contact person for each customer or lead. With digital lead nurturing, we're at a point where that one-to-one relationship can be closely replicated. It's a significant advantage to have solid lead nurturing programs in place where you can retain contacts that may not be at the right stage of their buying cycle, and work to improve your relationship with them.

The Give-to-Get Equation

The goal of the lead nurturing campaign is to share your knowledge, to help your leads and to earn their trust. This is the perfect opportunity to give to your audience and establish the principal of reciprocity. Digital marketing has always been a give-to-get equation, and your lead nurturing campaigns are the perfect opportunity to share education, resources and your time with your potential customers.

While you're sharing this knowledge and information, you'll also be learning more about your prospects. As you gain more information about their attributes and needs, you can move them into more targeted and compelling lead nurturing programs where you'll be sharing your expertise. At the same time, you'll be strategically soliciting response and feedback to help identify their questions, concerns and feedback. This feedback becomes extremely valuable as it can provide signals as to their location within your product buying cycle.

Another goal of your lead nurturing campaign should be to create affinity and trust with your potential customers. Lead nurturing campaigns are typically email-based with the goal of having a person-to-person dialogue. It's within this dialogue that you'll share information about yourself and look to help your leads. The trust that is built during this communication will also help raise your company's profile.

The ultimate goal of lead nurturing is to turn cold leads into warm leads that are ready to buy your product or service and turn satisfied customers into raving fans. Not every one of your leads is going to be a good fit for what you are selling, so it's important for both your organization and your leads to have an honest dialogue to help better understand the best path to take.

Lead nurturing is typically a very highly personalized, one-on-one communication via email. Lead nurturing rewards persistence, as it typically takes a minimum of seven touches to convert a cold lead into a sale. The nurturing emails are scheduled for delivery with anywhere from days to weeks in between.

This email dialogue begins with having a highly segmented email list based on the information that you've collected about your audience. For example, you'll want to know exactly what type of product or service someone in your list might be a candidate for or has shown an interest in.

All subsequent lead nurturing campaigns will then be strictly customized around the specific product or service a lead has focused their attention on. The goal of lead nurturing is to create the most customized, beneficial email dialogue possible to assist in evolving your relationship through the know-like-trust factor.

Lead nurturing is a constant data collection process. You are continuously sending out information and monitoring the response that is received. Once a contact opens an email, clicks on the link, responds to a poll request, or reaches out with more questions, you now have additional information with which you can customize your next email.

It's always helpful to think about how you would structure questions and responses within your lead nurturing campaigns as if you're going to have a direct one-on-one dialogue in person. As you learn more about your lead you can provide better information, better service, and more efficiently evolve your relationship.

A big part of lead nurturing is the process of transferring your expertise and knowledge to help educate your potential customer. Inherently this process lends itself to building trust because you are sharing before receiving.

An essential component of lead nurturing is identifying and monitoring *activity signals* throughout your lead nurturing campaigns. Your goal is to be able to identify where your lead is on their customer journey at all times.

If they know a lot about your product or service and are informed about your industry, they should receive more advanced knowledge products. Conversely, if a lead is new to this entire process, then they probably can benefit from a crash course in your discussion points.

The Four Stages

A major benefit to lead nurturing through digital marketing is that it allows the opportunity to guide leads through the buying process. There are four major stages to consider throughout the buying process as it relates to lead nurturing.

1. In the beginning, we are *collecting data* to identify the proper tracks or email nurturing workflows in which a lead should be placed. This process often begins with limited data, but with each step and in each stage of the lead nurturing campaign, we look to add more information and clarify the correct path for each lead.

2. The second stage within lead nurturing consists of *education and identification*. The information content that you'll be providing will trigger responses from your audiences that you can use to continue to evolve your relationship and illuminate the next potential steps.

3. The third stage is *monitoring the responses* you get back throughout this entire process. Is your prospect ready to be moved from a stagnant to an active state of demand?

4. The final stage of lead nurturing is the *transfer from being a cold to warm lead* that should be followed up with by the appropriate department within your organization. At this stage you've done your job—for now. You helped build the relationship and hopefully have created enough of a bond that the sales process should be fairly direct with a high probability of success. Once a lead becomes a customer, your post-sale lead nurturing campaigns begin with the goal of turning that customer into an evangelist for your product or service.

Stay Organized!

Despite the tremendous upside, there are many challenges within lead nurturing that you'll encounter. It's essential to manage the relationships in your lead nurturing campaigns with a culture of respect. There's a fine line between being too pushy and being too relaxed with your expectations and your goal for advancing the relationship.

Staying organized and keeping your database of contact data intact is imperative to match the exact communications with your leads. Your knowledge of their interests and their responses is the key to success. However, if you lose your organizational structure and you lose your ability to keep your data quality at the highest level, you risk destroying all your previous positive efforts.

It's also essential to work with your sales team or next level responders to help assemble the proper criteria for identifying active demand signals from your leads. The sales or customer relationship managers deal with your audience on a consistent basis. Their expertise can be a great source of information to identify the keys and clues that you'll be looking for when deciding who's ready to be qualified as a warm lead.

Lead Scoring

One of the most important tools that digital marketers have to identify warm leads is *lead scoring*. Lead scoring ranks each of the leads in your funnel and help you determine those that are the highest priority.

To determine a lead score, you'll use explicit data such as company size, segment of the industry, the job title of your lead, and their geographic location. You'll also use implicit data such as how many pages a lead has visited on your website, how many reports they've downloaded, or how many emails from you that they've clicked on.

From this data you can create a system to give a numeric score to the relevance of the lead's responses. The score for each lead will help you identify the spectrum of warm through cold targets in your database.

Lead scoring can be a huge benefit for digital marketers and especially small and medium-sized businesses because it allows you to treat each lead differently. For example if you identify that a contact has a high lead score, you can fast-track that lead and help them avoid a slower buying cycle.

Lead scoring can help achieve a smooth hand-off between being a marketing qualified lead and a sales qualified lead. It also helps identify the inactive or poor candidates in your database so that you limit your time investment and focus on creating relationships with the best potential candidates.

Marketing Automation

Marketing automation products are integrated, multichannel programs that help manage, optimize, track and aggregate customer engagement. With a marketing automation tool, your organization can better manage all of your marketing channels with much less time required than if you would do each individual component manually.

FOR THIS BONUS ONLINE CONTENT VISIT
walterlis.com/resources

As marketing automation platforms have become more intelligent and more robust, organizations are faced with deciding how much capability they need in this type of tool versus the investment required. For most small and medium-sized businesses, this will be the key decision, as you will need to decide how much of a tool you'll need to best manage and achieve your goals.

One of the key functions of marketing automation tools is the development and analysis of marketing campaigns. When you're creating a marketing campaign, an organization is typically looking to develop and execute a single campaign that will reach many consumers. With marketing automation tools, you can create a single campaign and have it become customized for each individual lead or customer. This is a powerful capability that just a few years ago was not within the grasp of a small or medium-sized business.

With a marketing automation tool you can also manage your marketing campaigns across all platforms. Having this ability to monitor, optimize, and improve your programs with feedback from real-time data allows organizations to stay quick and nimble, while helping them get the biggest bang for their buck.

Another key function of marketing automation is its ability to manage customer data organization and storage. As your customer database gets larger and the data that you collect becomes exponentially more diverse, managing all that customer information can become a major challenge.

Add customer buying and intent signals, and you'll see that there is a great deal of pressure to keep your customer database organized and optimized.

So what exactly is included in a marketing automation platform? There are three primary core capabilities for most marketing automation tools.

1. Nearly every tool has an email marketing engine, which allows you to create, send and track your email marketing campaigns.

2. Most marketing automation tools offer website visitor tracking capabilities. This is an important statistical area to track because this type of data can lead to an immediate indicator of buying cycle intent, such as responding to an email, visiting your website or spending time on a specific webpage.

For example, if you send out an email marketing campaign about your latest product, and the potential customer clicks on a link within your email, spends significant time on the landing page, and then forwards the link for that page via social media to their friends, you have three different signals of intent that allow you to determine whether this person may be a good candidate for an immediate follow-up conversation.

3. The third core capability of marketing automation is a central marketing database, and many times a direct connection to your CRM tool. I've used marketing automation tools as their own stand alone database and I've used them with direct integration with CRM tools. In either scenario, the better the integration, the better the results. However, if you have a CRM tool that may not integrate directly with your preferred marketing automation vendor, then you can usually manage both independently and effectively.

Beyond those three core capabilities, there are a number of additional capabilities that marketing automation platforms can provide. Many offer a blogging platform that you can utilize to replace or take the place of your current system.

Some marketing automation tools offer social media publishing and monitoring capabilities. This is an effective way to combine multiple signals, allowing you to more strategically utilize your customer information database. For example, if you send out a tweet and one of your potential customers retweets it, you have another signal of intent, or at least target awareness that allows you to better judge customer lifecycle status.

Some marketing automation tools also offer search engine optimization management capabilities. This is particularly effective when you're focused on content marketing within your organization to help drive traffic at the top of the funnel.

Another additional capability is to create calls-to-action, or any form of banners, buttons, or links that provide intelligent response tracking. Most blogs include a call-to-action action banner or button immediately after their blog posts to generate response on a related target to that post. Having the capabilities to track the response to that call-to-action and then align it with each customer in your database can be quite powerful.

An important tool for all marketers is the ability to create landing pages or customized web pages to help promote a specific offer. Nearly all landing pages include a form to help capture contact data from potential customers in exchange for a lead magnet. By combining landing pages and forms, you can leverage your thought leadership to increase your lead database. You can also utilize this knowledge to begin tracking customer response and intent throughout your website, email campaigns, and all other marketing initiatives.

One final significant capability of marketing automation tools is *lead tracking, scoring and segmentation*. As you attract new leads into your database, you'll have the ability to segment these leads into relevant buckets and interests so that you can provide the right message for the right lead. As you assemble more information on their likes and interests, you can then create a lead scoring methodology to determine where each lead is at in their customer journey.

If an organization can afford a marketing automation tool, the primary benefit is increased marketing efficiency. Leveraging a marketing automation tool in the proper format can help an organization get the most out of its core capabilities by significantly increasing output while significantly decreasing time investment.

As we've mentioned, another major benefit of marketing automation is enhancing the ability to generate more and better qualified leads. Since you're able to create customized offers and incentives you can attract the customers who might be the best potential audience for your products or services.

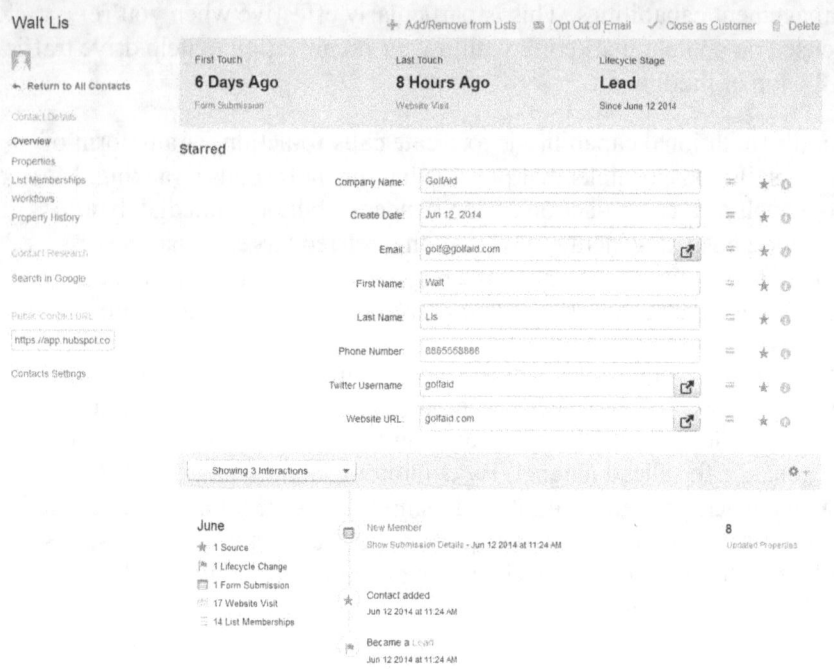

Marketing automation can also provide a multichannel view of prospect behavior that would otherwise require a great deal of manual time and effort to assemble. Marketing automation tools could be considered at the forefront of the big data movement to help not only collect data but extract the insights and potential opportunities that all of this customer interaction can provide.

Marketing automation can also deliver better alignment of sales and marketing goals by refining the message to your audience in much greater detail than was previously available. The good leads are now all the leads, as we're able to create and manage more efficient and effective communications and see better results that we can consistently track.

With solid marketing automation and lead nurturing, we can also improve our lead conversion and return on investment. ROI should be the key driver in any marketing tools investment. Not only will you be working to increase and improve the quality of leads that you're attracting, but you'll also be warming up those leads so that the conversion process is enhanced greatly.

Challenges of Marketing Automation Tools

Although there are many benefits of marketing automation tools, there are also some challenges involved. One of the primary challenges is that they can be somewhat time-consuming to calibrate and setup at the outset. Depending upon the platform and the familiarity of those involved with setting up the tools, marketing automation implementation and on-boarding can range from a few days to a few months.

Also, if an organization does not invest in utilizing all the features of the purchased product, the marketing automation tool can become a glorified email marketing engine. This underutilization should never be acceptable. The key features of each tool are a significant part of their investment and it's incumbent upon any organization to learn how to learn and leverage these assets.

A final challenge of marketing automation can be internal organizational resistance to changing marketing processes. This type of resistance can impede platform adoption and efficiency, if a group or groups within the company is slow to adapt.

That's why it's important to have a united front and consensus across all segments of the business before the implementation of a marketing automation system. The different stakeholders within each organization may have questions or concerns about the product. It's advisable to clearly explain the benefits, capabilities and goals of a marketing automation tool to help everyone understand the system and how they can better achieve their goals.

When choosing a marketing automation platform, it's recommend to take an extensive inventory of all current marketing processes. Understanding how you communicate with your customers and how this type of the tool can assist will help not only decide what you should purchase, but how you can best leverage it to improve your results.

It's also essential to know how you're going to measure success with this type of a tool. Are you looking to drive more qualified leads from the top of the funnel to your organization? Are you looking to better capture more information about your potential customers and better share that data with your sales team? Are you looking to become more efficient at nurturing your leads, whether they're digitally generated or come through off-line channels?

Begin to identify where you're looking at for improvements within your marketing. Establishing your goals for what you want to achieve will help dictate not only what to purchase, but how to implement this type of system within your organization. Marketing automation can be a huge game changer for any small and medium-sized business, but as with all digital marketing, if it's not implemented properly, its impact can be significantly muted.

Chapter 10

The Marketing Audit

In order to define your organizational growth and improvement priorities, it's necessary to have a crystal clear picture of what you're trying to accomplish. There are many potential objectives that you could have for your marketing, so it's essential to decide what's most important and what comes first.

1. Set Marketing Goals and Objectives

The first step in creating your marketing audit is to identify the marketing goals and objectives of your organization. For example, are you looking to increase awareness or visibility for your company? Or, are you looking to increase visibility of a particular product or product line? A goal like this could lead you to creating a demand generation component within your marketing to help your potential audience become more aware of what you can do and how you can help them.

Another goal could be to increase the size of your current audience, or to acquire an entirely new audience. A byproduct of a goal like this would be to generate qualified sales leads.

You may be interested in activating your audience by getting people to take a particular action such as participating in a contest, downloading a file, or registering for a webinar. This type of audience participation is helpful when looking to invigorate the vendor/customer relationship.

Some organizations may be looking to increase the retention rate of their current customers. In this case, a wise intermediate goal would be to increase communication with your existing audience by sharing your expertise and providing value.

If you're looking to get referral customers, a relevant objective would be to get your brand evangelists or happy customers to recommend you and to solicit new business on your behalf. In order to get to this point, you'll need to understand what people are saying about you and become aware of the sentiment within your marketplace.

The majority of marketing goals and objectives for most organizations, especially small and medium-sized businesses, is to drive more sales and revenue. In order to accomplish this, we must drive more people into your store, whether it's bricks-and-mortar or online.

A final potential goal is to build a community by connecting with other like-minded individuals. Building a community is a great way for any organization to enhance their reputation and aid all other parts of their marketing.

2. Define Your Customers

After defining your goals and objectives, the next step is to describe your current and ideal customers. In order to create the most clear buyer personas, it's essential to understand who these people are.

By collecting as much data and information as possible about your leads, it will help your marketing plans enormously as we look to align your marketing messages to reach your target audience. Important lead data would include job titles or functions, geographic location, company size and their social media participation. Being able to identify their background, familiarity with your industry and overall awareness of your product or service would also be greatly helpful.

3. Define Your Product or Service

The next step in your marketing audit is to describe what you're selling: your products or services. We need to know exactly what the features, benefits, purpose and distribution looks like for all of your products and services.

What are the individual strengths and weaknesses of your offerings as compared to your competition? Are there any legal, technical, economic, or governmental factors that may affect the industry that you're working in? For example financial organizations typically have rules and regulations that are established by the governing boards within their industry for product or service marketing.

It's also helpful to understand the current industry awareness of your organization as well as its products and services. Do other companies control the particular brand or term for what you're selling? Or are you well recognized and at the top of the mind of the potential customers that your selling to?

And finally what is your estimated share of the market for each of your products and services? Has this changed drastically over time, especially within the past few years?

4. Review Your Marketing Efforts

The next stage of your marketing audit is to describe your current and past marketing programs.

• Exactly what tactics have you tried?

• What's worked and what hasn't?

• What advertising and promotional vehicles have you tried, such as print, broadcast, out of home or online advertising?

• Has your organization had success with PR or media relations?

• Do you attend or exhibit at particular trade shows, special events, seminars?

• Have you used market databases or tracking systems to target customers?

• In addition to all of these tactics, what have you not tried but have considered within your marketing plans?

• What have your competitors been doing to grow their business?

5. Identify Competitors

After taking an inventory of your marketing programs, our next step is to identify your top competitors. What are the differences between you and your competitors in terms of product features, benefits and sales distribution methods? Where does your competition rank in terms of sales or market share?

In terms of digital marketing, which of your competitors has a solid social media presence? Who ranks at the top for your related keywords? Which organizations have a high degree of online authority? What does their backlink profile look like? And finally do they have any link magnets on their website that are attracting an audience?

6. Review Your Digital Campaign

The next stage of your marketing audit is to focus on your own digital marketing priorities. What is the current reach, or exposure that you're receiving across all digital marketing channels? How well do you rank on search engines for branded, category and industry keywords? What do your email marketing programs look like? What kind of response do they receive?

Do you have a presence on social media channels relevant to your organization? Are you running digital advertising campaigns? If so, through what traffic providers? Are you involved with affiliate marketing?

7. Analyze Your Digital Architecture

The next stage of your internal digital marketing audit is to focus on the structure of your digital architecture, including marketing channel design and functionality. Is your website easy to use and accessible to search engines? Is your site mobile friendly? Does your site load quickly or have any broken links? How well are your social media channels and networks working together?

Do you have a content strategy for your organization? If so, who are the primary stakeholders within your organization to create content or is the content creation being outsourced? Are you creating content for all of your targeted audiences?

Are you creating valuable link magnets and lead magnets to attract attention and potential customers to your website? In what formats are these assets available? Text? Video? Photos?

Are your digital marketing channels being optimized, or are they in "set it and forget it" mode? Do you have email marketing workflows in place to funnel customers towards the most appropriate tracks? Is your website optimized to attract potential leads and retain their interests? Do you have a clear call to action within your social media presence?

Are all of your marketing channels, both online and off-line, being successfully integrated? Do your off-line and online marketing campaigns complement one another? For example are you promoting your appearances at trade shows with promotion on your website, digital advertising, and all other marketing materials?

8. Measuring Success

The final element of your internal marketing audit is to identify how well you're measuring the objectives and metrics for your digital marketing performance. Do you have an easy-to-use system for collecting and reporting data to the stakeholders within your organization? Do you have goals and objectives that are clearly available to compare the results of your programs? Do you have reporting protocols in place? Are these reports analyzed and acted upon?

Creating the Marketing Plan: Six Goals

There are six overarching goals to consider when creating your marketing plan.

1. Systematize Whenever Possible

Among all of your resources, your time is typically the most valuable. Therefore, it's imperative to maximize this resource by creating systems to simplify and improve your processes and make them more efficient. Try to avoid "recreating the wheel" within your marketing efforts by reusing processes whenever possible.

2. Utilize Organizational Knowledge to Earn Trust and Awareness

The strength of most small and medium-sized businesses is the expertise and experience of its employees. The goal of your marketing should be to identify and share this internal knowledge to help your customers. It's also a great way to earn trust and awareness from your audience.

3. Leverage Existing Resources to Maximize Return On Investment

When developing your marketing plan, you'll need to utilize the tools and resources you currently have available to build your audience and to help grow your reach to the next level. Most organizations can get more from less, simply by becoming more efficient with their technology, processes and human resources. Building upon your existing resources is an effective way to get the most out of your investment.

4. Attract a Relevant Audience

The reality is that having the *right* audience is usually much more important than having a *large* audience that won't ever be potential customers for your business. In fact, your marketing challenge can be amplified if you have a large but unsegmented audience that may not be a candidate for what you're selling. Yet you'll eventually need to identify and exclude the poor lead candidates, consequently creating more work and resources necessary for your organization.

5. Create a Roadmap for Your Audience

Your goal when developing your marketing should be to guide your relevant audience through tailored email paths based on their lifecycle stage. What this means is you need to create email workflow roadmaps for each buyer persona. Throughout these workflows, you also must be able to identify buying question patterns so you can determine what stage of the customer lifecyle a lead is in.

6. Convert Your Leads Into Customers

Driving revenue is the primary marketing goal and objective for most small and medium-sized businesses, and therefore converting leads has to be always considered top priority.

So what are some key strategies that we should consider when developing a marketing plan? From the outset, by creating a plan we're already ahead of the overwhelming majority of businesses, who typically take more of a reactive approach. However, there are five key strategies to consider that will help you get the most bang for the buck within your marketing campaigns.

1. Track - Track the response from all of your marketing efforts whether they be digital or off-line so that you can gauge success and failure. Digital marketing especially makes this easy and imperative.

2. Optimize - Look to constantly optimize and improve the systems and processes within your marketing. Organizational advantages occur when companies are able to "squeeze the most juice out of the orange" by optimizing all of the components of their marketing.

3. Capture - The beginning of our customer relationship starts with capturing marketing qualified leads that are solid potential customers. Without leads, our marketing efforts will be restricted to a secondary role.

4. Nurture - A strength of digital marketing is the ability to nurture marketing qualified leads into sales qualified leads. Creating email workflow tracks and paths to help educate and build trust with potential customers is a major advantage of today's digital marketing.

5. Grow - Quite simply, the job of marketing is to help grow the business by expanding the quantity and quality of our leads, customers and business relationships. Digital marketing is the lynchpin to help grow these relationships and to help expand the reach of your entire organization.

Chapter 11

Explaining the Process

We've covered all the individual aspects of digital marketing for your small or medium-sized business. Now you need to explain to your organization how the system works. In this chapter, we'll summarize how all the moving parts come together to achieve your goals.

There are four primary steps that comprise the process of turning a website into a business development machine. Each step builds upon the previous one, creating a chain reaction that helps trigger growth.

1. Create Awareness

The first step to establishing your business and identifying growth prospects is to create awareness of the website and the digital presence of your organization. By using traditional digital marketing tactics such as search engine optimization, paid advertising, content marketing, social media marketing, and email marketing, your objective is to build your audience and create awareness.

2. Identify Your Visitors

There are three primary visitors to your website. The first is the person who says, "Yes, I want to buy your product or service now." These people have found your site and have identified that you can provide them what they need at this point in time. This group has a clear agenda and are at a point in the buying cycle where they've become comfortable identifying what they need.

From a marketing perspective, your mission with this audience is to remove as much friction from the potential purchase. Whether it's offering them a link to a form on your website, a button to buy now, a link for an email conversation, a phone number to talk to someone directly, or the ability to have an immediate online chat, your job is to make their intended purchase as simple and easy as possible.

The second possible visitor is the person who somehow made it to your site but will never need your product or service. They may have found your site through search or clicked on a link, but mistakenly have arrived at your doorstep with no current or future need for anything that you can offer. The best alternative for both of you in this case is to limit the time and resources spent to extend this relationship.

The third and largest group of visitors to your website are what I call "the Maybes." These folks found your website, and have an interest in what you can offer, but they aren't yet ready to buy and need more. They may need to learn more about your product or service. Maybe they need to learn more about you in your organization. Maybe they need more time before their budget becomes available.

The Maybes make up the overwhelming majority of people who visit your website. That's why it's essential to put the primary focus of your marketing efforts on winning over the Maybes.

3. Convert the Maybes

Step three is to convert the Maybes into leads. We've identified that the Maybe visitors to your website are potential investors in your product or service, but they're not ready to buy yet. Therefore, it's your job to make sure that the Maybes don't come for a visit and leave without identifying themselves.

If someone clicks on a link to your website and is a potential customer, allowing them to leave without knowing anything about them does not help your business grow. It also doesn't help the Maybe who could use your help and assistance.

We use three primary tactics to convert Maybes to leads within digital marketing. Firstly we use landing pages to exactly align each visitor with their desired product. For example, if you sold bicycles and a visitor is looking for information about a part for their bike, your goal is to immediately get them to your bicycle parts area.

Secondly, we use forms to capture visitor information. Learning who the Maybes are, by gathering their email address at the very minimum, is the best way to help this potential customer and assist them in finding what they need. However, if they visit your website and leave without identifying themselves, the chances that they'll return to your website are poor, despite their new found familiarity with you. Potential customers have an enormous number of options at their fingertips, so once you have someone, you can't afford to let the relationship disconnect before it gets started.

The third step in converting Maybes to leads is to use a valuable offer or "lead magnet" in exchange for their contact information. We call these types of offers lead magnets because they help attract relevant potential customers to your website. A lead magnet typically comes in the form of a free report, white paper, product discount, free demonstration or a free consultation.

It's imperative that your lead magnets provide a tremendous amount of value in the eyes of your customer or potential customer so that they're willing to exchange their email address for what you're offering. A best practice in creating and managing your lead magnets is to test multiple offers to see what potential customers find valuable. Once identified, you can leverage these offers throughout your site to help attract and turn more Maybes into leads.

4. Nurturing Leads into Sales

This fourth and final step requires turning the leads that you've captured into sales with a process called lead nurturing. At the highest level, lead nurturing is building a relationship, in this case, primarily through email, with a potential new customer.

The first stage of nurturing a lead into a sale is identifying who they are, what they want, and what they know. By finding out this information you can begin to identify and establish what topics and types of information might be of assistance to this lead, and allow you to begin building a relationship with them.

The second stage is to use what's known as *email workflow tracks* or *drip campaigns*, which consist of a group of emails sent over a period of time, that help educate and build the relationship. Our goal in this stage is to create a highly customized sequence of emails that begin to build a conversation by providing value every step of the way. The more we know about a lead, and what stage of the buying cycle they're in, the more focused and valuable information we can provide.

The third stage of this process is to build a relationship, establish trust and convert these relationships to sales or sales ready leads. A typical lead nurturing campaign consists of anywhere from four to ten emails that are sent every few days and help enhance your credibility with the lead.

It's important to realize that just as building a relationship in a face-to-face or real-world manner takes time to establish trust, the same is true for digital communication. We can't jump steps or try to shorten the process because the relationship has to evolve at its own pace. We can certainly do our part to speed up the process by paying attention to the feedback and buying signals of our audience, but we always have to be cognizant of the comfort level of the lead.

The Golden Question

When talking with small and medium-sized businesses about how they approach their marketing, I often refer to the "golden question." This golden question is the same one that has been asked in bricks-and-mortar stores since the beginning of time to any person who walks into a store. The golden question is, "How can I help you?"

This simple question that I'm referring to is where vendor/customer relationships have started for hundreds of years. And the reality is no different in the digital realm as we look to identify where our business can help a potential customer.

Reminding yourself of the golden question throughout all digital marketing processes will help you stay on track with the goal of assisting your customers and providing value to everyone you come in contact with. Each email that you create, each web page that you build, each conversation that you have, it's essential to always remember the golden question of, "How can I help this person?"

Reference Notes

1. http://www.sba.gov/sites/default/files/FAQ_Sept_2012.pdf
2. https://www.census.gov/hhes/computer/files/2012/Computer_Use_Infographic_FINAL.pdf
3. http://www.pewinternet.org/2012/06/06/main-report-15/
4. http://www.pewinternet.org/fact-sheets/mobile-technology-fact-sheet/
5. http://www.marketingcharts.com/wp/online/in-the-us-time-spent-with-mobile-apps-now-exceeds-the-desktop-web-41153/
6. http://moz.com/google-algorithm-change
7. http://moz.com/rand/the-t-shaped-web-marketer/
8. http://whichtestwon.com/
9. http://digitalmarketingcalculator.com/
10. http://w3techs.com/technologies/overview/content_management/all/
11. http://www.nytimes.com/2012/03/01/technology/impatient-web-users-flee-slow-loading-sites.html
12. http://visual.ly/role-web-hosting-your-website

Index

About the Author

Walter Lis is a digital marketing consultant, writer, conference speaker and small business owner with a passion for creating and executing successful online marketing strategies. His core technical expertise includes search engine optimization, digital advertising, email marketing, social media marketing and web analytics.

Prior to starting his own marketing consultancy, Walter gained over 20 years of experience working for businesses ranging from multi-billion-dollar companies to sole proprietorships. Walter has held senior management positions for The Chicago Tribune Media Group, sports information provider STATS, LLC and investment management firm Attain Capital Management. He's worked with companies in a wide variety of industries including media, publishing, telecommunications, manufacturing, local government, information technology, construction, and finance.

To contact Walter, please visit him at www.walterlis.com.

www.ingramcontent.com/pod-product-compliance
Lightning Source LLC
Chambersburg PA
CBHW051332170526
45166CB00002B/781